The most powerful word
In the Universe

John Bullock

DEDICATION

To those who have gone ahead and before, who have made the Word of God the final authority in their lives. I salute you and have learned so much from the experience that you have passed on. I am indebted to those who have pioneered, made their stand and taught a message of faith. From my heart, I thank you.

CONTENTS

INTRODUCTION

What you are about to read began life in 2002 as 'The Royal Law.' It was truth, put down on paper that had transformed my life. In fact it rescued me from what I believed was a terminal illness and a very dark place indeed. In the first part of the book you can read all about that time. However, that was then and this is now. I have continued to build on that revelation and learned that one of the Biblical words used for love (there are four) is, when understood and importantly applied, the most powerful word in the Universe. Of that I have no doubt and don't think that you will either when you recognise just where the Greek word *agape* appears in Scripture. For example: in 1 Corinthians 13 described as the great love chapter, each time the word love appears it is translated from *agape*. The word is the power of God, primarily it is something we receive, is meant to be something we live by and when we do we can learn to use in our every day lives. *Agape* describes the highest form of love; it is love at Gods level. Scripture declares that God is *agape.* It is so important to God that he commands us to do it. In it is the power to redeem, reconcile, restore and resurrect that which otherwise would die. Only *agape* can truly resurrect. If there is a simple way of understanding God, his purpose, the reason for Jesus and the empowering of Jesus' followers, it is understood through *agape*. It is no wonder that the Apostle Paul had this to say, *"The only thing that counts is faith expressing itself through love (agape)."* Galatians 5:6

I believe that once understood you will see that *agape* is the key that unlocks all other keys of the kingdom. Through my own journey I have experienced the outworking of this, culminating in our ministry now in Tanzania: AGAPE LIFE. The more we live in *agape* the less we fear, the more we love the more authority we have. *Agape* is the doorway through which we must pass to experience in every day reality the following: *"He (Jesus) replied, 'I saw Satan fall like lightning from heaven. I have given you authority to trample on snakes and scorpions and to overcome all the power of the enemy; nothing will harm you."* Luke 10:18-19 *"all the power of the enemy,"* means just that! So does, *nothing will harm you.* Imagine living like that? Well you can! It is my aim that by the time you have read and applied the information in this book that you will walk a fearless path, knowing you have the authority to overcome everything you face on your journey through this life. At the same time increasing your productivity in reaching this fallen world through the power that is *agape*. I have learned and pass on to you when *agape* is lived it can also be used through the spoken word. It is the most powerful word in the Universe and a lethal weapon that is available to every child of God. It is time to awaken this truth in your life and take off into living in a new dimension. Sooner or later, every believer hears that words have power. In this book I aim to convince you of that truth and my prayer is that you will learn, in practice, how you can, *bind and loose* on earth with your words and grow into a realm where you can "*say to your mountains, go throw yourself into the sea, and do not doubt in your heart but believe that what you say will happen, it will be done for you.*" Mark 11:23

John Bullock
Arusha, Tanzania 2014

CHAPTER ONE
AND SO IT BEGAN

"He who began a good work in you will complete it
until the day of Jesus Christ."
Phillipians 1:6

Everyone knows that television blurs the senses but this was TV unlike anything I'd ever watched before. I was not unused to examining my heart, in the spiritual sense, but never before had I looked at it from the inside. It was February 2001 and I was on the operating table in Wythenshawe Hospital, Manchester, undergoing a procedure called cardio-ablation. Level with my chest was a screen to stop me from seeing the lower half of my body and, to my left, were raised TV monitors. I was wide-awake and I could see and feel the instruments that were inside my heart to isolate the weakness so that it could be ablated. I had never been through anything like this. In a sense, the operation, as I see it now, had begun a few months earlier, perhaps several years earlier, but we can start in North Wales. It was the year 2000.

Deb and I and the kids were in Prestatyn, in Wales and we were making our first trip home from Africa in two years. Even after just two years, it was quite an adjustment to get used to the pace and way of life in the UK. We were attending the annual UK conference of the Elim Pentecostal Church and it was a time of high excitement for us, particularly seeing many old friends and colleagues. We had with us at the conference Ayhubu Mgweno, chairman of Elim in Tanzania and Simon Githigi, chairman of Elim in Kenya - two men who had become very dear to us. Ayhubu, sadly passed away in 2012.

During the afternoons, I was attending the business sessions where the ministers and lay leaders meet to discuss business and the way forward for the Elim movement. On the Wednesday, we were discussing finances with regard to evangelism and mission in general. I felt troubled in my spirit. I had recently been with the two men from East Africa in Rwanda amongst the aftermath of genocide and my overall perspective had been influenced by what I had experienced in East Africa. I felt that I needed to bring a point of view into the meeting of some 450 leaders, but, having never spoken at a business session at the conference before, I decided to wait, ponder over my thoughts and pray.

The next day we were discussing pensions and I knew, in my spirit, that God wanted me to speak. I handed in my slip (the normal procedure) and sat back down feeling unusually nervous. I waited patiently but wasn't called by Wynne Lewis (Elim's General Superintendent at the time) who was chairing the session. I interpreted it to mean that God didn't want me to speak and went back to my seat somewhat embarrassed. However, a little later I was called and I was given a very warm welcome, as this was our first leave from the mission field.

As I began to address this large gathering of leaders, I fumbled at first. I went on to genuinely thank those who worked behind the scenes with pensions and such but I wanted to draw attention to a man who had served the movement for 41 years in Tanzania. He had served diligently often without any money at all. Ayhubu Mgweno owned nothing that we would consider valuable. He didn't own his own home, had no car, no computer and certainly no pension. Even though he was nearing retirement, he still travelled around East Africa by bus, visiting different parts of the work. 'He has nothing of real value in this world materially as I have but I'm in awe of him' I remarked, my voice rising and full of emotion. I drew more attention to him and asked that we might gain some perspective.

After about ten minutes, I finished and sat down. The place was hushed and the presence of God, tangible. I can only describe what happened next as remarkable. Many commented afterwards that God's presence was awesome and that it was a defining moment for our denomination. Ayhubu was called to address the gathering. Into the dramatic hush he merely whispered 'I think everything has already been said'. With this, I was as surprised as anyone to find myself prostrate on the floor at the front of the auditorium - I was weeping aloud and uncontrollably. Then our incoming General Superintendent, John Glass, asked if he could clean Ayhubu's shoes with his handkerchief. Many people began to weep and prostrate themselves.

One man came from the back of the auditorium and took off his shoes and wristwatch and placed it on the platform at the front. A gentle stream of people laying down money and private possessions followed him. Business was now postponed as Simon Githigi addressed the crowd. God's presence filled the building. In that short period of time, God honoured Ayhubu with several thousand pounds, with intent to buy him land, build him a house and provide a pension. In addition, the plight of our overseas workers would be reviewed. He had made no appeal and sold no merchandise but God knew his plight. I had no idea that God was going to do such a thing. I was merely hurting in my heart with regard to what I knew to be the reality of service for our third world colleagues. When you consider the average wage in Tanzania, at that time, was $130 per annum you will get some idea of what I had experienced.

What happened that day to bring the manifest presence of God into that meeting? I cannot say for sure but obviously I have analysed it over and over in my mind and feel that I have some answers.

This book is the result of a long and, at times, painful journey but will shed some light on what God has shown me. Even though I was indirectly involved that day, I can honestly say that in all my time in the church and ministry, I have never experienced anything like the presence of God that filled that building. I had experienced God moving powerfully before, but this was different. It was tangible and an obvious lasting work was in motion. Certainly in my own life this has proven to be so.

Meanwhile, I could have had no idea, then, of what was to follow in the next few months. The following few pages are a brutal account of what went on and the lessons I learned through it and up to the present day.

CHAPTER 2
AN ACHING HEART

"Above all guard your heart for it is the wellspring of life."
Proverbs 4:25

After a great summer ministering around the Elim churches in the UK and spending as much time as possible with family and friends, we returned to Africa on the 2nd August 2000. As we landed in Nairobi, it was a good feeling to see the sights and smell the scent that is peculiar to East Africa. It had been wonderful to be home in the UK but we agreed that Africa now felt like home.

We had so much to catch up on with colleagues and friends in the ex-pat community, so much work to do into the future. Our role was to oversee the Elim work throughout East Africa, which consisted of Tanzania, Rwanda, Uganda, Kenya, East Congo and Burundi. Our area was many times bigger than Britain and this in itself made the work seem impossible. It was an endless stream of dire human need - at times incomprehensible to our western values and lifestyles. The security issues made it almost impossible to live out some romantic dream such as living like the Africans do in the bush. We were working amongst the poorest of the poor but living in a nice home even by western standards.

There are many paradoxes in Africa: it was once described as a lot of lovely people doing unspeakable things to one another. Many times I had lost myself walking and praying around our hometown of Arusha, contemplating the enigma that is Africa. It can lift you up and it can bring you down swiftly, suddenly and destructively.

Because we had relative wealth (our income was about £16,000 per annum) and would be targets for robbery we had learned to live with 24 hours haskari (guards) on our fortress like property. We also had guard dogs roaming; all this to protect us from those we had come to serve and to reach. It was something that one got used to, eventually.
The truth was that, without these measures, you would be violently robbed; it was not merely a possibility, it was a certainty! As a

family man - our children, Chris and Beth were 8 and 6 at the time - one could not take such risks. Desperation and the ease in which a person can get hold of guns is quite a potent recipe. Many of our friends had suffered armed robbery.

There were so many desperate needs surrounding us that we were often completely overwhelmed. The queue of needy folk was like an endless stream - exasperating. It seemed like we had to put a guard around our hearts so that we could maintain some normality as a young family.

Often I would be away for weeks at a time driving endless miles to reach various parts of our work. There was such variety: I could find myself in a refugee camp one week, an executive meeting the next and famine relief soon after. Through it all, I was never quite sure that this was God's bull's-eye for my life. Overwhelming is not an adjective that is too emphatic for what we faced. Despite all this, it is true to say that Africa does get in your blood; she is like a lover who lifts you up with delightful promise only to dump you, suddenly. Frequently, The missionary feels very undervalued in East Africa in the sense that whatever endeavours he or she undertakes on behalf of the indigenous population, it is usually only what is expected and this is swiftly followed by a request for more. The 'begging bowl' is quickly emptied. It often seemed to me that I was not simply trying to meet the needs of a village but rather that of several nations. The following are two accounts from my diary that show the ecstasy, the elation and the frustration of working in Africa.

11th March 2000, Ngara refugee camp, Western Tanzania

'This was one of the most amazing days of my life. We visited the refugee camp at Ngara. Both the trip and the time spent there was fantastic and memorable! The crossing of the bridge over the Kagere River where so many genocide victims were disposed of was a stark reminder of what went on here. The tremendous welcome of the Burundian pastors and people in the camp (they had been waiting five days for us) was remarkable, the great anointing of God breaking out spontaneously on the people. The sights we saw. The miracle of getting back across a closed border and the singing and

fellowship in the packed vehicle on the way back - what a day! A million thanks Lord for the way this day has affected my heart.'

10th January 2000, Soroti, Uganda

'The demands of this job are far too great. The Africans are looking for an administrator to sponsor them and their expectations far exceed mine or even Elim's ability to meet them. How can one person even begin to administer this major operation?'

Many times when I try to make clear how I feel to the Africans, their response is non-plussed. I don't think they can begin to understand how we Wazungu (white men) feel. I am not even sure that culturally (with all that has gone on historically in Colonial days) that they want to love us. We can be used by them... The problem is we do not have anything like the money they think we have. Even if we did, it would be morally wrong to dish it out like candy. Our only hope is to build strong churches in the cities and give some indigenous example to the rest of the work. Another problem is that we are not in a place long enough to have any kind of relationship with our people. We flit in and flit out doling out the shillings as we go. The shillings are never enough, thus, greatly undervaluing all we are seeking to do. The mission field of East Africa has become a pariah even to the degree that the pioneer missionaries who gave so much, are almost blamed for the attitudes of the present day Christians, 'They gave us something material in order to preach the gospel to us', some Africans reason. Nowadays, that mindset is so engrained, that is has become a very big stronghold.

What can be done when the African church (in some instances) will sell out to the highest bidder among the organisations from the West? The truth is there are some naive and, may I say, unscrupulous ministries that will offer the 'candy' in order to add to the books.

There can be no doubt that we, in Elim East Africa, are facing a formidable stronghold. At present, I do not think that we have either the resources or the personnel to bring this thing down. Accordingly, the frustrations are enormous. We certainly need more resources but surely they must be provided indigenously? I must have an understanding of what can be expected with regard to tithes and offerings into the head offices of each country. I may not fully understand the ins and outs of all that this entails but the principle remains: Elim in East Africa must be built on Scriptural principles and not be swayed by enduring circumstances.

We must develop communications (at this time we do not have one computer amongst all our workers in all of Elim East Africa). There should at least be a network uniting all of the head offices. We should also consider putting short-term workers into each head office to observe and to minister under the supervision of Elim UK. Two week visits can be very productive but may also leave people with a false impression and therefore be counter-productive.

As it stands we simply do not have either the practical or human resources to advance. It is a full-time job simply to maintain. We cannot and should not underestimate the spiritual resistance and subsequent pressure that this places on one person. We should project by faith but can only manage to work within the set parameters that present circumstances allow. Advancement that does not have its origins in God is no real advancement at all and will, at some stage, be paid for by someone. God is only interested in reality and not in how something may look from external observations. The fact remains that Elim in East Africa has expectations that far exceeds the ability of Elim in the UK to meet. Each country is constantly presenting needs that far outweigh the entire budget for the whole region. To compound this, most of these needs are genuine and, in some cases, desperate. We could spend our entire budget, our entire salary and still not scratch the surface in meeting one need in one country. Such is the frustration!

We cannot single-handedly solve the problems of what is, after all, a region of third world countries. Of course we do not act alone but I think it behoves us to ask serious questions of what does God expect from Elim within the complexities of all that is East Africa. The shear geographical size of the region (many times bigger than Britain); the poor, at best, non existent at worst, communications and the extreme poverty ought to cause us to face a re-think. The 'shaking of the tree' mentality is coped by most only at village level (literally). We have to cope with it at a multi-national level. Only one who has faced the African way of shaking the tree can begin to understand the pressure that this brings to bare. 'Overwhelming', is definitely the right word! Help!'

As I have just said, my life moved from feelings of elation to feelings of great frustration. This is normal for missionary work and is one of the things that can make it different from ministry in the West. This was certainly the case for me with the role that I had.

However, as we progressed through the month of August 2000, I was feeling fresh and encouraged and made the long journey down to the city of Dar es Salaam in Tanzania. I went to meet my friend and supervisor from Wales, Denis Phillips. We had a few meetings in Dar before passing through the town of Tanga where we had scheduled more meetings. We then set off on our long drive to Arusha to prepare for our first East Africa Leaders conference. We had a great sense that we were breaking new ground and God was moving on our hearts through the deep conversations we were having.

On the 21st August, the leaders arrived from around Tanzania, Uganda, Kenya, Rwanda and one from the refugee camp that I had visited in Ngara in Western Tanzania. Back in Arusha, it was with excitement and enthusiasm that Denis and I ministered to the 20 or so key leaders that had gathered together. The main theme of my teaching was taken from Ephesians 3:14-21, while Denis brought revelation about the gifts of the Spirit. Not for the first time, Denis and I were in tandem and tremendous things were happening. We finished on the Saturday and, after loving farewells, we almost collapsed with exhaustion! On the Sunday afternoon we met with what we called our "afternoon group" who were, in the main, fellow missionaries. As Denis ministered effectively into this close group of friends little did I know that a few hours later I would be unconscious.

I had been suffering some palpitations and they were keeping me awake that night. I went to the toilet at about 1.30am feeling weak and faint. As I was leaving the bathroom, I collapsed and lay in an unconscious state for some time. I came round with a bloodied head and I went back to our bedroom to wake Debbie - she phoned a missionary doctor who was a good friend and speedily drove me to a clinic in town where I spent the night. I was assured that I hadn't had a heart attack but that I had a severe irregular heartbeat. This was confirmed a couple of days later as I underwent extensive tests in Nairobi, Kenya.

Dr. Patel, the consultant, informed me that as I had both a fast and slow heartbeat, it was fairly complicated and the treatment would require both medication and a pacemaker - the medication to slow the heart down and the pacemaker to make sure it wouldn't slow down too much. The decision was made to go back to the UK. A few days later we were back in the UK in Blackpool with Deb's parents and, soon after, I was taken into the Accident and Emergency at Blackpool's Victoria Hospital where they managed to stabilise my condition in what was, to me, the 'scary' Coronary Care unit. After a few days, I was released and, for several weeks, I went back and forth to the hospital and eventually I was advised to have, the, afore mentioned operation, called cardio-ablation. As I was feeling fairly good at this stage it was decided that we would return to Africa and later on I would come back to the UK to have my operation. Thus, we met with Denis Phillips and our Missions Director, Brian Edwards, to discuss the finer details of the plan. The meeting went well and it was with some excitement and not a little relief that we drove back to Deb's mum and dad's.

That evening I went to see my GP and he told me that my consultant had communicated that he wanted to change my medication from Sotolol to Flecainide. He issued me with a prescription and dutifully I began to take the new medication - little did I know that a near fatal mistake had been made.

The following night I felt my heartbeat slowing to a point that I knew my life was in danger. The next morning I called my Doctor who said that I had to persevere on the new medication. By Friday I was in a terrible state and was amazed to find out from my consultant that I should have come off Solotol two days before I started the Flecainide and that in Blackpool the procedure was to go in as a day patient to be monitored on the effects of the Flecainide.

By Sunday, I was back in Victoria Hospital, Blackpool as an emergency case - my heartbeat was between 180-200 beats per minute in the resting position. Later in the week it slowed to a dangerous 22 beats per minute, yet through it all I felt God's hand and at peace. After nine days I was transferred to Wythenshawe hospital in Manchester where I underwent the cardio-ablation procedure.

It was one of the strangest experiences of my life.

The procedure involves passing a few tubes into the main artery in the groin. Through these tubes instruments are passed into the heart, where they open out and go to work in an attempt to locate the weakness. Once the weakness or extra passage is found, it is then burnt out or cauterised. All this takes place while the patient is wide-awake. It is possible to watch this entire procedure on screens by the side of one's bed. Not nice! It was, however, effective but what happened in the following months became a nightmare, as my whole system seemed to dysfunction.

To begin with I began to suffer chronic insomnia to the point that I could no longer sleep naturally. I could not even catnap or fall asleep even for five minutes. I quickly became exhausted and was sure I was dying. In addition, I would sweat profusely for no apparent reason; even taking a warm drink would cause me to be drenched through perspiration. Later, my digestive system could not handle food and I began to pass meals, seemingly undigested. During this period I suffered different pains all around my body including migraine and I was rapidly losing weight. The period over Christmas was a sad and desperate time. In the early hours of Christmas Day I penned the following words in my journal.

My beloved family how I love you all, and need you, I can't begin to tell you the torture and torment that is going on inside me at the moment. I have taken so much for granted and now it seems I have lost it. How I plead with God to give me another chance to get back to normal living. My mind is in such turmoil. My need of sleep and rest is obvious. Deb, you have been my dream girl from when we first met- how sorry I am that it has come to this! What a partner you have proven to be, God knows I never deserved somebody like you.

Thank you for standing by me through these troubled days. How fortunate I am - I ask you to remember the real me and pray that we will have a miracle of restoration. How I wish I could be me and join in the Christmas festivities wholeheartedly - my lack of sleep is dampening my enthusiasm because of the prospect of tomorrow.

Only God knows if there is a way forward out of this mess? I need help and am so grateful to have a loving family around me. You have all been better than words could describe. The fruit shown by your mum and dad have proven them to be giants in my sight. Thank you Chris and Beth. I plead with God that He will allow me to share your tomorrows - you are fantastic my angels. Words cannot describe how I feel about you all. I have been very fortunate as I look back and think about the amazing times that God has given us. Oh that he will give us more in the future. In the service on Christmas Day as I sat at the back of the church I was so proud to see your ministry Deb - you really have something special in God and you looked so radiant. The hat makes you look very beautiful indeed (you have just told me to write good things- I was as you can see) it is a privilege to be your husband. You know that I have always felt that but certainly during these days of my illness I have so appreciated every touch - every chance to hold hands- every cuddle.

Remember when we first met and went out, how precious every touch was, every look, every letter (where are they?). We can safely say that we have never lost our romance, have we? It has always given me a tingle to be in your arms - even the slightest touch has been precious to me always. And the joy of producing two fantastic children together- surely they are amazing! (Wouldn't any proud father say that?). Chris and Beth I just want to write the words, I Love YOU. Deb, I want to write these words, I Love YOU. I have to nip myself when I consider that I am married to you. I mean it from the bottom of my heart when I say you are, to me, the greatest, most ideal woman in the world. That is how I have always seen it. Every parting has been a desperate time until we were back together again. God grant us tomorrow and may our tomorrows be even greater than our yesterdays!

I was writing as a man who had lost all hope (I have since learned that a Christian is never truly in that position) and really felt that each day would be my last. I can happily testify that God answered that prayer from a desperate heart. The fact that I am rewriting this book partly in Tanzania reflects that fact. It is hard now to read that entry into my journal without tears welling up.

One thing I have realised since my illness is that I thought, during it, that I was thinking normally and using my usual analytical thought processes. I now know that I was not. The worst thought was that God was punishing me. My mind was in turmoil and I was under enormous stress. Consider that our home and possessions were still 5000 miles away in Tanzania. We simply had no security and no direction for the future. The stress became visibly obvious on Debbie and from time to time the children would tearfully ask, 'Daddy, when are we going back to Africa?' I simply felt that death was imminent and worse that I would end up in hell! My mind was so stressed. We were in turmoil and I felt like I was under pressure, literally, 24 hours a day. I didn't want to die but I seriously thought that my family would be better off without me.

On December 28th Debbie, in quiet desperation, phoned Denis Phillips to ask if he could help me. That day I travelled down to Swansea to be the guest and 'patient' of Denis and his wife, Ronaldine. Once again, I was about to be overwhelmed by love and kindness. They gave their time, energy and decision-making over to me - this included setting the daily agenda and even choosing the daily menu. I was experiencing God's *agape* (unconditional) love through people at precisely the time when I thought I didn't deserve it. Daily, Denis took me to spots around South Wales that had become familiar to Deb and I over the years. One day we went down to the seafront at Mumbles and the next to the beautiful resort of Tenby.

Another of the days that will stick in my memory forever was a day when I noticed that the Chinese meal I had eaten the evening before had been passed through my system undigested - this fact served to compound my fears. As Denis and I walked on the beach at Oxwich Bay on the Gower I reminisced about the times that Deb, the children and I had enjoyed there during better times. I felt just like I imagined the condemned man must feel on death row. I felt that my life was over and I could only plead inwardly that God would restore me and give me another chance (my frame of mind at the time didn't really allow for that possibility but I have now been back to Oxwich Bay on several occasions with my family) back then I was a desperate man!

On New Years Eve in 2001, I sat in Denis' home like a Zombie. Denis continued to fill my mind with positive thoughts but it was hard to take them on board. After about a week Deb and the children arrived. I went to see them wearing a new haircut and dressed in a new suit that Denis had bought for me. I took Deb for a romantic meal at the Watermill restaurant at Ogmore Vale, near Bridgend, she was looking particularly lovely and that night was one of the most amazing of my life. It was like our first date. In the midst of our prevailing circumstances we could only trust God for the future – on this occasion my trust had to go way beyond my human hope.

We spent the next few days at the Phillips' house counting every moment as precious. During those days I was shocked when Denis asked me if I would like to preach at Porth, the church we had pastored before moving to Africa, on the coming Sunday. I had not preached for months and initially I thought it impossible. Nevertheless, Denis convinced me to go and I eventually agreed.

As Sunday morning arrived (after another sleepless night) I wondered what on earth had inspired me to agree to go and preach! I felt awful on the journey and as we entered the Rhondda Valley, via Trebanog, memories of the nine mostly happy years we had spent there came flooding back. Tears welled up in my eyes as we arrived in Porth and we were given a tremendous reception from the folk in church. When the time came to preach, I spoke from my heart on the subject of suffering and, at the end of the sermon, many people came forward to pray and lay hands on me for healing. Although I didn't realise it at the time, we had just experienced our beginning point.

After the meeting, we went for lunch at the home of John and Jill Price who had been like surrogate parents to us over the years. John had been an Elder for many years in the church and, along with Jill, epitomised the outliving of the Christian message – they were truly dependable with massive integrity. As a family we had grown to love them dearly, they were like rocks to us.

After the usual scrumptious lunch at the Price household I asked John if we could speak in private. He became one of the three people I opened up my heart to and confessed my known sins. I was convinced I needed to carry out the injunction in the book of James 5:16,

"Confess your sins to one another and you will be healed."

I thought that maybe this was the obstacle to me being restored (as previously stated I was so desperate and feeling that I had been abandoned by God) so if it was the obstacle, I was going to do all that was in my power to remove it. That afternoon I went through sins, some of which I had committed up to fifteen years previously, and confessed years before but I wanted to make sure that I was forgiven. Poor John sat and listened and tried to bring comfort to me. I was a haunted person and felt prepared to go through any humbling just to recover from my (imagined) fallen position in Christ. John was a great help to me that day. John Price went to be with the Lord in 2011. The earth's loss was heaven's gain! A legend had gone.

I didn't know then as I know now, that sin and law come at the believer hand in hand. The effect of the law on those who have little conscience has only a silent, unknown, yet devastating affect, whereas, it serves to bring a sense of immediate condemnation into the believers life – one who is in reality no longer under the law. The guilt, turmoil and torment of the Christian often has no substance outside of a believers thoughts but the thoughts can be so powerful that they take life upon themselves. I have learnt that this is true in a positive sense as well as a negative one. The law has its most devastating effect in the thought lives of those who are striving to be "pure in heart". We left the Rhondda that day oblivious that God was about to perform an amazing twist in this ongoing tale.

Later in January, Debbie and I went to meet with our superiors again. At the meeting, in the Imperial Hotel, Blackpool, we were told that we would not be going back to Tanzania (I was already reconciled to this). The news was devastating for Deb – I think she had not come to terms with what was, at the time, a foregone conclusion. It was a dreadful meeting at which I remained speechless while my darling wife broke her heart. As far as I was concerned she was suffering because of God's displeasure with me.

I felt I was an imposter, how much I needed to learn some basic foundational truths about the nature of God, even though I had been in the ministry for many years. In short, my soul had not been sufficiently restored.

As the meeting concluded, we made a swift decision to travel back to Wales to stay with some friends. In later days, we would recount how I sat in their lounge once again resembling a Zombie. After another sleepless night I paced about the room trying to concentrate in prayer. Eventually, I felt God was speaking to me in my thoughts (the manner in which I had been accustomed to over the years) saying we should move back to the Rhondda Valley. The second thing I heard was that we would have to climb a mountain, but, when we arrived at the summit, we would be at a place that few people arrive at.

Debbie and I chatted over this latest revelation and somehow it took root within us. At the very least we could settle back into a familiar area where many of our friends lived and where our children had spent their earliest years. Later that day I spoke to Denis Phillips and he said he would support our decision. It was the first day of a remarkable chain of events – we had definitely boarded the vehicle of recovery.

In early February we moved back to South Wales and stayed with other friends at their home in Pontypridd. They offered us wonderful hospitality and kindness. We quickly settled Chris and Beth in new schools and I began some voluntary work with my friend Phil Davies, who was the Communications Director of Newport Rugby Club. Phil, along with Carl Brettle, had formed a

Christian company to facilitate the growing opportunities afforded by the Internet.

It was an exciting time and, by now, I was getting some sleep due to the effects of a previously untried sleeping tablet called Zopliclone. We began to settle back into life in the valleys of Wales. I was still living one day at a time but seeds of faith had sprung into my heart. I began to receive hope through the means of faith. As the days went by, I began to deal with things completely by faith. In other words, I disregarded my feelings, learning that though my situation was reality, I could, through faith, attack it with a **higher reality**. What a lesson this truth, gleaned in 2001, would go on to be to this day.

A few months earlier on 29th November 2000, I had written these words in my diary:

"Trying circumstances sometimes look as if they combine for a person's destruction – they do not, they only combine for the destruction of the self-life and then the working out of the Christ-life from within him."

Later I would learn that if we believe the truth, obey the commands and claim the promises then, eventually, our position in Christ would overcome our condition in the world!

Gradually, (though not without setbacks) this began to happen. What a lesson: unless you are certain of your position in Christ, it is highly likely that you will give into your condition in this world. I needed to understand that amazing grace as opposed to just grace, as I had understood it, would radically change my outlook and, as a result, my life and the lives of multitudes of people. I learned that the important thing is to make contact with God until you can find what I described as a, 'beginning point' and then to walk hand in hand with the Lord until the victory is manifest. Hope is born in understanding that simple procedure. Most effectively, I learned that God's mercies are new every morning.

So, here we were settling back into the Rhondda Valley but still our home and possessions were in Tanzania. One Saturday I was invited to speak at a Prayer School led by Jenny Grant who had worked with us in Porth for a number of years. It was at the School that one of several domestic miracles took place. It was there that a man called Allan Jones approached me. Allan was one of the leaders at Providence Church further up the valley. He told me that the church had a house that was empty and that we could move in straight away if we wanted to. I told him we were interested and, after viewing the property, we moved in. As I write this we have lived rent-free in the house for two years (shortly after I wrote this the house was given to us). About this time we were also supplied with a car (free of charge) from Phil Davies. Things were indeed looking up or at least someone was looking down.

As my health improved we began to feel confident to go back to Tanzania and settle our affairs there. By faith we decided to plan to go in June. However, before this happened something amazing took place. The Porth church, that we had formerly pastored, was experiencing some difficulties with division in thinking amongst the leadership (I mention this in relation to what will follow). We had previously known little about this but could see that the situation was grave. Many of the people who were involved had been with us during our time as pastors there and the whole situation between the present pastor and some of the leaders was in danger of splitting the church. It was difficult to sit back and watch this happen but we no longer had a say in matters and I had been too ill to even think about it.

As a few weeks passed by, the situation worsened and, out of the blue, the present pastor announced that he was leaving to take up a new position in the North of England. No one had had any idea that this was about to happen. He had given his notice to Elim HQ in September 2000. Immediately, I was asked to return as pastor.

It would be possible to read all kinds of things into these happenings but God knows that no one in the church, least of all Debbie and I, had any foreknowledge of these events. In May 2001 I was inaugurated back into the pastorate. We took the facts that Deb and I had never lost our love for the Welsh Valleys, and that I was a Welsh speaker, as confirmation that this was to be our next step. We can only look back and ascertain that God took hold of our lives and worked through the events that you have just read about.

On 17th June we went back to Arusha and had a memorable time seeing our friends and tidying up our affairs. It had been unexpected, to say the least, after our emergency departure some nine months before. I felt well and was greatly looking forward to our new challenge in Porth.

I have a good imagination but I could never have written the script for what had taken place and the terrible events of the previous year that would act as bedrock to teach me, in practice, at a level I had never previously been to.

I trust that as you read on, the insight I have gleaned will find rest in your heart and bring revelation to you. I can thank God that my experiences have led me to walk in a new dimension that has continued to expand to the point that I feel confident to teach the life transforming subject matter of this book. Here you have my offering, may it do you the power of good.

CHAPTER 3
FOUNDATIONS

"That you being rooted and established in
love (agape) may have power"
Ephesians 3:17-18

Our re-installment into Porth was not popular with everyone and a few people left. We soon found that many people were hurting deeply due to their interpretation of events among the leaders, so we had to know more about what it meant to love one another at God's required level. For years I had been seeking to understand the subject of keeping the Royal Law based on the scripture found in Matthew 22:37- 40 and James 2:8

In order to understand the rest of this book, it is important that I introduce you to one of the New Testament words for love taken from the Greek language. That word is *agape* - meaning the highest form of love, unconditional in nature. *Agape* is a love that can only come from the being of God.

It is a love that loves without changing. It is a self-giving love that gives without demanding or expecting re-payment. It is love so great that it can be given to the unlovable or unappealing. It is love that loves even when it is rejected. *Agape* love gives and loves because it wants to; it does not demand or expect repayment from the love given. It gives because it loves, it does not love in order to receive. It can be defined as a sacrificial, giving, absorbing, love. The word has little to do with emotion; it has much to do with self-denial for the sake of another. It is not based on feelings.

Jesus replied: " 'Love (agape) the Lord your God with all your heart and with all your soul and with all your mind.' This is the first and greatest commandment. And the second is like it: 'love (agape) your neighbour as yourself.' All the Law and the Prophets hang on these two commandments."

In 1996, I penned the following words believing them to be from God,

'The world has yet to see what can be achieved through a people who are fully committed to living out the Royal Law whilst at the same time embracing the full dynamics of the faith.'

How I had longed to be part of something like that – it was a dream. I have learned that sin is not the obstacle to this revolutionary living because sin has been dealt with at the cross. The obstacle is self or the self-life. We must die (to selfish living) in order that we can live! There are a number of obstacles, namely: doubt, pride, self-life and fear, all of which can be devastating.

I knew that the fact Jesus commanded us to *agape* meant that we should give it more thought than we had. I had previously pondered much on this; it was a subject that had niggled in my heart for years. I began to ask some questions of the Lord and He began to give me answers.

During my illness, it seemed like my whole world had fallen apart. Obviously my foundations had been flimsy in the hour of testing. It is easy to see that now, but, as previously stated, I was unable to think straight while under such stress. It is now obvious to me that, like most people, my faith had not been properly grounded or consolidated during my early years as a Christian.

All the knowledge, understanding and experience gathered in life can only be absorbed into the foundation of what we are in essence. Right foundations, therefore, are imperative. The Scripture tells us that we must be rooted and established in *agape*. I want to remind you again that we are purposely using the Greek word, *agape* to translate love to continue to emphasise the point of the book.

Coming to Christ gives us an opportunity to re-establish our foundations but, sadly, most Christians don't and I was one who found it really difficult to accept myself and to understand that God doesn't stop loving us when we fail Him.

We know that God is in covenant with us but do we fully understand what that means? Recorded in the book of Ephesians are two prayers prayed by the apostle Paul. The latter is found in Ephesians 3:14-21:

"For this reason I kneel before the Father, from whom His whole family in Heaven and on earth derives its name. I pray that out of His glorious riches He may strengthen you with power through His Spirit in your inner being, so that Christ may dwell in your hearts through faith. And I pray that you being rooted and established in agape, may have power together with all the saints, to grasp how wide and long and high and deep is the agape of Christ, and to know this agape that surpasses knowledge – that you may be filled to the measure of all the fullness of God. Now to Him who is able to do immeasurably more than all we ask or imagine, according to His power that is at work within us, to Him be glory in the church and in Christ Jesus throughout all generations, forever and ever! Amen."

I knew full well that Christ dwells in our hearts through faith – but I didn't know that the more faith we have, the more He dwells. Faith is substance even though it can't be seen. This means that faith is as real as the things that are seen. However, it is impossible to operate in this until you have understood what it is to be rooted and established in *agape.* When you think about it, how can we?

"And I pray that you being rooted and established in agape, may have power together with all the saints, to grasp how wide and long and high and deep is the agape of Christ, and to know this agape that surpasses knowledge – that you may be filled to the measure of all the fullness of God."

It is possible to be, *filled to the measure of all the fullness of God?*

This measure is linked to our understanding and application of loving at God's intended level. Don't read over that quickly.

We are to be, *rooted and established in agape.*

I cannot stress enough the above statement.

Then we need to grasp: *how wide and long and high and deep is the agape of Christ, and to know this agape that surpasses knowledge.*

Furthermore, we need to grasp this when we first come to Christ and not at some future date after the devil has used our lack of knowledge against us. Be sure that our enemy, Satan, wants us to get used to Christianity at a much lower level than this.

In my own situation, I had been undone good and proper and the manner in which I was sinking should never happen to a child of God. I had been badly deceived by the evil one and it had worked a treat but now it seemed like I was daily learning new truth about building a proper foundation in Christ.

Sermons on this subject were coming fast and furious and, in private counseling, I was like a child with a new toy trying to show individuals what God had given me. In terms of my health, there were good and bad days but now I had stopped interpreting the bad days as God's displeasure with me. This was an enormous breakthrough to bring me out of darkness. It is easy to write about this now that my mind has been transformed but I want you to know that if you are going through such a battle, I really can empathise and, if you apply what I am saying, you will recover. You will!

So, if it's really possible to be, *filled to the measure of all the fullness of God,* then it is the answer to everything. Evangelism, non-verbal and verbal would take care of itself. It dawned on me very clearly that we couldn't continue to ignore God, in regard to His requirements of *agape* and then expect Him to move among us, and our communities in Biblical proportions.

There is now no doubt in my mind that God has three priorities for our lives:

1) We are to love (*agape*) the Lord our God with all our hearts, minds and strength.
2) We are to love (*agape*) our neighbour as we agape ourselves.
3) We are to love (*agape*) one another as Christ has loved us.

These words are vitally important – with, as and as.

We are to agape the Lord our God **with**...
We are to agape our neighbour **as**...
We are to agape one another **as**...

This seems to be such simple teaching but I have been around long enough to know that we are generally missing it by a great distance!

The question is: do we agape according to the above clauses? That is to love no less than at God's intended level?

All of the Law of the Prophets hang on these things. That means everything else is dependent on us understanding this truth and applying it to our lives. We think that we do love and we do, but by this world's standards. Rarely are we 'loving' at God's commanded level.

Please note that we are dealing with commands here, these are not good ideas or requests. What can we expect from God if we ignore His commands? As someone who has served in the armed forces, I fully understand that there are dire consequences in failing to obey a command.

At one particular time in my career in the Navy I had to be part of a special unit of 26 men made up of Navy and Royal Marines personnel in Northern Ireland. It was in the dangerous days of the mid-seventies. Our role was to try to stop the gun-running activities of the IRA terrorists. It was a very precarious job and not a pleasant six months of my life but I had no choice but to do it – I was under command. Disobedience carried extreme consequence, particularly as I was on active service. I have learned that despite God's unending love for us disobedience to His commands is self-harming; it carries serious consequence. Ouch! God has given us clear commands concerning love.

One Sunday morning as I ministered in Porth, God showed me clearly that we couldn't do that (perform miracles or bring to bear the power of God in a situation) until we had done this (loved at His commanded level). It was simple but it was clear. I remember walking through a doorway to illustrate that there was a whole world of God's goodness and power through the door marked "Royal Law." I could see clearly that the goal of every Christian life should be to develop the character of Christ – this is why we should spend time with God, not so that we can bring Him a shopping list of prayers, rather, so that we can develop His nature and fulfil our obligation to keep the Royal Law. If we walk through the door marked "Royal Law" we will find another door marked "Revelation Knowledge." This latter door will be opened to us in its uncorrupted state.

I was beginning to see that for the past few months, I had been living through the first part of Psalm 23:

"The Lord is my shepherd I shall not want, He makes me to lie down in green pastures, He leads me by quiet waters, He restores my soul. He causes me to walk on paths of righteousness for His names sake."

In the midst of Him making, causing and leading, He is restoring. It had been a hard, nightmarish journey, but I am now writing what you are reading.

He wants to restore your soul too. When? Right now: as near to the beginning of your Christian walk as possible. Don't waste another day! Today and not later you should learn who you are in Christ!

"Be transformed by the renewing of your mind." Romans 12:3

If we are to *agape* God with all our strength – then we must be restored into His image.

a) We need a changed heart.
b) We need a renewed mind.
c) We need a restored soul.

Then we can *agape* Him with all our strength because we are not wasting energy in a needless direction. That's why He *makes*, *leads* and *causes*.

He *makes* me to lie down in green pastures, He *leads* me by quiet waters and He *causes* me to walk on paths of righteousness for His names sake.

Has God led you into (or at least allowed) the situation you find yourself in today? 'No' you cry, He couldn't possibly, it is so horrible. Well yes... but you must understand that God does everything from an eternal perspective. The situation I found myself in was a nightmare but much of the defeat that I felt inside could have been avoided, if I had been rooted and established in *agape.* My worst fear, during the illness, was that God had given up on me, even to the point that I was now going to hell. I had a very muddled mind but the thought felt real.

Have you ever felt that you have blown it completely or that you have committed the unpardonable sin? If so, you are not alone – certainly not alone! Indeed you are in good company but the fact is you have yet to understand God's **amazing** grace, which means the greater the sin the greater the grace. For me, it wasn't that I thought I had committed the unpardonable sin but my inability to rationalise God's hand on me when I was in such a state. The truth is: you will never be able to adequately love others until you have realised how much grace is available to you.

'You can never fully receive others until you know that you have been fully received yourself.' Henri Nouwen

No doubt, like me, you have a problem interpreting God through how you feel or the circumstances you find yourself in. Consequently, the enemy will find it easier to tilt you off balance. You are more secure than you think, my dear friend! It is not so much what happens to us along life's journey; it is more important how we interpret what happens in us along life's journey.

E+R=O (author unknown)

Event plus response equals outcome. Not the event but how we respond to the event. And we will interpret these happenings according to the foundation that we are looking out from. Can we ask: what can I learn from this in order to mature? I learned a long time ago that God is more concerned with our maturity than He is with our temporal happiness. Happiness is a state we will experience forever. For now, however, we can expect a few blips but even during the blips God, our Father, is never far away. He is:

"An ever present help in times of trouble" Psalm 46:1

But I've learnt, with time, that the more mature and complete we are in our faith the more joy we will experience.

And, in James 1:3-4, we are encouraged by the following:

"Consider it pure joy whenever you face trials of many kinds because the testing of your faith develops perseverance and perseverance must finish its work so that you are mature and complete not lacking in anything"

It is imperative that you know that God wants all of His children to be in this state, *not lacking in anything*. Every temporary trial is designed to bring a lasting blessing. Being blessed is only achieved as we meet God's conditions but these conditions are not to be a futile attempt to keep the Law. No, the Law has been made obsolete for the child of God. You are free but, if you want to *lack nothing*, then you have an obligation and that is to, *walk in the Spirit*. I don't want to complicate this because it is achieved when we *agape* at God's intended level.

If this becomes the goal of our lives, then we will be both fulfilled and effective for God. We have to realise that He expects us to work at this and holds us responsible because it does not come naturally and needs determined cultivation. I had wanted this state for years but there were so many weaknesses in the area of my soul that it seemed impossible. How can you walk in love at this level when you won't believe that God loves you at this level? You can only possibly give *agape* to the degree that you have allowed yourself to receive it. You should be looking up far more than you are looking down; you should be smiling much more than you are frowning – how Satan wants to fill your mind with negatives!

God dwells in the believer's heart so the key to life is allowing Jesus to be released from within. This is what had happened in that extraordinary meeting at the conference in 2000. One of the biggest mistakes we have made, generally speaking, is not seeing the seriousness of consolidating new believers. Until we are rooted and established in *agape,* we will be limited because we can only do that (miracles and the extraordinary) when we have understood and applied this (*agape*).

Are we too busy trying to find out things that we are not sure of, to the degree that we are ignoring the things that are obvious? Could it be that God is saying, 'I am not telling you anything else until you do what I have already told you?'

"Seek first the Kingdom of God and His righteousness and all these things shall be added to you." Matthew 6:33

One thing that is clear in the word of God is, God didn't say 'seek first the church!' He said, *Seek first the Kingdom...* The church is part of seeking the Kingdom but whilst it may be possible to exhaust all that the church is, we can never exhaust the Kingdom. The fact is, we either listen to the word of God or we hear other voices - the mind is not neutral. We have a choice but, due to neglect, most of us are listening to voices other than the word of God.

However, it is clear:

"Man does not live by bread alone but by every word that proceeds from the mouth of God" Matthew 4:4

We gain further instruction on this in Proverbs 4:20-21

"My son, pay attention to what I say, listen closely to my words. Do not let them out of your sight; keep them within your heart; for they are life to those who find them and health to a man's whole body. Above all else, guard your heart for it is the wellspring of life."

King David was chosen because of the condition of his heart. Satan's attempt is to harden your heart so that he can stop you at source by nullifying the wellspring of life. Has he succeeded? The seed of life that God places within us is both creative and unending.

Faith based on love means that nothing is impossible for those who believe. Satan is well aware of that fact so he does his utmost to spoil it by hardening our hearts. The heart is hardened whenever we walk in un-forgiveness and bitterness, which are, by nature, a lack of *agape*.

We have access to supernatural provision and the means of this provision is faith but you can't understand that until you understand this; you will not walk in revelation knowledge, thus, maximizing answered prayer, unless you love at God's intended level.

The doorway then to supernatural provision is to keep the Royal Law of *agape*.

Have you ever wondered why God doesn't just appear to His followers? The answer is, we can achieve more by understanding and applying faith than we could by seeing God. Faith is the outworking of revelation knowledge, which is far superior to the knowledge that comes to us through the senses. The Lord does not often appear because His appearance would be interpreted by the senses whereas His word is interpreted by revelation knowledge. Faith is more powerful than sight - we have not fully understood what can be achieved by faith. We pass through a doorway into another realm by loving at God's intended level and through that door the spirit realm provides all that we need. It is an exciting and an obtainable place to all believers.

"The only thing that counts is faith expressing itself through love (agape)." Galatians 5:6

The Bible clearly speaks about a realm where believers can dwell, where we can achieve incredible things by faith, a place where we have authority over the evil one. It is a place of supernatural provision where God sends heavenly gifts.

The problem is, I repeat for emphasis, you can't have that until you have done this!

Until we are rooted and established in "This *agape*" we can't pass through the door where the realm of the spirit is a manifest,

---

continual reality. But, once you have decided to keep God's commandments on *agape*, He opens up this dimension to you.

Faith can only be received from another world. Once we are certain that we have God's word on a situation, something incredible happens, we can speak it into being:

"You shall say to this mountain..." Matthew 21:21

The problem is, most believers unnecessarily remain at the wrong side of the partitioning wall because we try to do this before we have done that. Can you understand? So often we make no real attempt to keep the Royal Law but try to walk in positive confession in order to activate the promises of God. Now you know why we remain relatively powerless!

Listen! God is not a liar. His word is true but there is a reason why we are not experiencing it in its fullness.

Let's face it, we have been sold an untruth that trying to cast out devils, heal the sick, devise plans to reach the lost or soak in the Spirit (all valid things) are more exciting than it is to work at loving at God's required level.

We must adopt normal Biblical practices that result in supernatural consequence.

Don't live for one moment longer under the wrong perspective – God has provided everything we need for both maintenance and growth. He is still able to create on our behalf. Make no mistake, it is God's intention that we come to a place in Him where we can speak to situations and change them. God is saying to us, if you will *agape,* then, you will also do all that is promised in my word.

Severe harm can be done in an instant and all that is needed is a tongue. Severe good usually takes longer, until we realise we have authority to break Satan's power in a person's life by using our tongues alone! Start now by deciding you will not settle for less.

———

CHAPTER 4
BEGINNINGS

"God's mercies are new every morning."
Lamentations 3:23

Through vast amounts of personal study and a variety of experiences, I have concluded that the most important thing in our dealings with God is how something begins. The wonder of the Christian life is that we can begin again and then if necessary begin again. God's mercies, are indeed, new every morning.

We can safely say that if something begins in God it will go on to succeed. With this in mind, I am very concerned that most Christians are not given the benefit of beginning well. As long as you have a good beginning, a solid grounding in who God is (an unwavering knowledge of His nature) and who you are in Him, you will have no problem in applying the following:

"We live by faith and not by sight." 2 Corinthians 5:7

"So we fix our eyes not on what is seen but on what is unseen for what is seen is temporary but what is unseen is eternal."
2 Corinthians 4:18

Remember, that in terms of Kingdom principles, 'If you can see it, it's not permanent.' The same is true of touch, taste, smell and sound. In other words, if it is communicated to you by the senses, it has no permanence. The things that are unseen are communicated to us through the Spirit.

It is the Spirit in a man that brings understanding.

Take heart in the following words:

"He who began a good work in you will complete it until the day of Jesus Christ." Philippians 1:6

If God begins something, we can guarantee that He will complete it.

The biggest question, therefore, is whether or not something has its origins in God or not. In other words, did God begin it? All that we have to do is find the beginning and make sure that that beginning is in God. What you need from God is a beginning point.

The principle of this is found in Genesis chapter one:

"In the beginning, God..."

And also in John 1:1

"In the beginning was the word and the word was with God and the word was God."

Because God began it, God will finish it. In the book of Hebrews we read of the great heroes of faith,

"All these people were still living by faith when they died. They did not receive the things promised; they only saw them and welcomed them from a distance." Hebrews 11:13

From a distance...

Faith will look into the distance. We must look beyond natural horizons. As long as you have walked through the door you will start to see what is beyond the door. And remember it is: loving at the commanded level that enables a believer to pass through the door. As we shall establish, faith does not come through seeing; it comes through hearing. We are called to see beyond what we see in the natural sense. And this kind of seeing does not actually come through seeing but rather through hearing.

I cannot say for sure when I found my beginning point that led me to be healed but I did find one and that's the important thing. I found it because I looked intently for it! If you can pass through the gate (the door) you will move from relying on what you see to relying on what you hear. What you see is determined by perspective what you hear is determined by faith.

I've learned, in terms of what you are seeing, nothing is as it seems.
In Romans 10:17 we are told:

"Faith comes by hearing and hearing by the word of God."

And in Galatians 3:5

"Does God give you His spirit and work miracles among you because you obey the law or because you believe what you heard?"

Faith is not faith unless its source is the voice of God speaking either in general or specific terms. God gives us advanced information so that we can act on it. So, if we are sick, we must determine what God is saying to us about our illness. If we have financial problems, we must hear what God is saying about them. We must hear what He says about marriage, child rearing etc. and then apply it.

I have been using the term 'beginning point' repeatedly because it is absolutely vital. I want to stress again its importance because if you can find that beginning point in God then the outcome is assured even if the answer is still in the distance. It will eventually draw near. We are assured of this because it is a universal law in God that if He commences, He also concludes.

Read that again - several times if necessary - until you have digested it.

Sometimes we can't perceive a good outcome because we haven't got the resources to achieve it. What we should do is seize the chance that God gives us and submit ourselves to His discipleship and He will provide the resources.

Every beginning, in God, has an end result that is favourable in God. That is why He can reassure us that,

45

"All things work out together for the good for those who agape the Lord." Romans 8:28

Your part is in the loving - cultivating the essential part of your relationship with God. You do have a responsibility:

"Therefore I urge you brothers in view of God's mercy to offer your bodies as living sacrifices holy and pleasing to God. This is your spiritual act of worship. Do not conform any longer to the pattern of this world but be transformed by the renewing of your mind. THEN you will be able to test and approve what God's will is - His good, pleasing and perfect will for your life." Romans12: 1-4

Without doubt, His will is to bless you and to see you become a blessing to others. In every sense He wants to resource you so that you are always in a position to carry out is word to: *do unto others what you would have them do for you.*

The same passage of scripture taken from The Message reads,

"So here's what I want you to do, God helping you: take your everyday, ordinary life - your sleeping, eating, going-to-work and walking around life - and place it before God as an offering. Embracing what God does for you is the best thing you can do for Him. Don't become so well adjusted to your culture that you fit into it without even thinking. Instead fix your attention on God. You'll be changed from the inside out. Readily recognise what He wants from you, and quickly respond to it. Unlike the culture around you, always dragging you down to its level of immaturity, God brings the best out of you, develops well-formed maturity in you."

How long should the new convert give into digesting and understanding the importance of this? The fact that it is easily bypassed is in large part a reason why we find ourselves impotent in the outworking of things of God. The promises of God are all in existence on your behalf. But they will remain distant until we meet the conditions that release the keys of the kingdom and bring the promises of God into our possession.

Faithfulness without on going obedience to God's directing is not enough. Faithfulness accompanied by obedience is what God is looking for. We should be left in no doubt: Faith leading to obedience is the key that opens the windows of heaven to release the blessings of heaven into the earth's atmosphere.

What parameters and horizons have we imposed upon ourselves? God wants us to see beyond those parameters and horizons. And if you have lost your way, you need to find a new beginning. All you have to do is find a beginning point and allow God to stretch you. I found one and it has projected me into a realm I had not previously experienced - without doubt, you can too! Search for your beginning point. It may take some soul searching, even a humbling.

Maybe your traditions or past experiences have imposed limitations on what you can believe God for. Well, perhaps it is time to ask why you are so limited.

We should ask more questions of what we have accepted. To quote a line from the movie, The Lion King, 'You are more than you have become!'

Focus for a moment on the following questions:

Why do we do what we do?

Why do we see it that way?

Why do we impose such limitations on ourselves?

In answering these questions, begin again. Find your beginning point in God.

How?

Do whatever is necessary to hear His voice for your situation. Maybe you need to go back to the point where you allowed a stumbling block to come into your life. Start today. Either way you need a spiritual answer. A new foundation can begin this very minute if you will talk with God from an open heart.

47

Here is a solid Biblical prayer to help you:

"Search me O God and know my heart. Test me and know my anxious thoughts, see if there is any offensive way in me and lead me in the way everlasting." Psalm139: 23-24

I repeat: all the knowledge and understanding that we glean can only be absorbed into the foundation of what we are in essence. Foundations, therefore, are imperative!

Dig some new ones today. I did and it has and is continuing to transform my life. Don't accept the status quo - it is not final.

Whoever you are and whatever you have done you can change and change is accomplished by one major decision followed by a series of choices.

'You cannot become what you are destined to be by remaining what you are.' John Pattendon

It is high time that we developed a new norm in the church of Jesus Christ.

We can still write the next chapter in determining the legacy we shall leave those who follow us. With all the resources of Heaven that are available to us may we decide conclusively to do so!

CHAPTER 5
THE SECRET OF ANOINTED SERVICE

"How God anointed Jesus of Nazareth with the Holy Spirit and power and he went around doing good and healing all who were under the power of the enemy." Acts 10:38

We should develop *agape* by making faith decisions because we will all have many tangible reasons not to *agape*. For example: it takes faith to leave justice to God rather than desire revenge. It takes faith to give precious time and money into the Kingdom of God that in the natural we can ill afford to give.

The Apostle Paul said in Philippians 3:3

"I place no confidence in the flesh"

And in Ephesians 6:10

"Be strong in the Lord and in His mighty power."

We must go beyond the flesh. During my illness, the day came where I realised beyond any shadow of doubt that I simply had to go beyond what I was seeing, feeling and imagining. Most importantly, imagining! Actively cast down your imaginations. Don't wait until they go away.

At all times we can rely on God's presence and strength at our time of need. And I believe it will be manifest to us in the area where we need it most. "When we are weak, then He is strong". As the songwriter said, "Now let the weak say I am strong". Agape has its greatest effect when it flows through human weakness. We are involved in God's work and He is always strong! Death is only an enemy when a believer's soul feels insecure. Otherwise it is most certainly a promotion.

Therefore, our main task is to find out what pleases Him and do it. We can be certain that the main way to please God is to fulfil the greatest command, to strive to *agape* Him with all our heart, soul,

---

49

mind and strength and then to *agape* for Him by loving our neighbour as we love ourselves. If we can become *filled to all the fullness of God* and then learn to release that life then God will surely do more than we can *ask, hope or imagine.*

Listen: hear me now, I repeat, as long as God's life is released He will do more than we can ask, hope or imagine and the glory goes to Him.

Imagine the degree of life you can release once you are filled to the measure of all of the fullness of God.

There is a vast difference between anointing and hype but, from the naked eye, they can look the same. The key to releasing the life of God from within is to understand the following: Jesus passes out of our beings into the atmosphere through the heart. However, the trapdoor of the heart (so to speak) can only be opened from the inside, in other words, by Him. It is not by human strength or by education or by hyping up a meeting; it is by loving at His level and determining right motives for service. Then, at the right time, He will manifest His presence.

Christian life is not about position or even location; it is about Him, our on-going relationship with Him. When that is in place, He will give the opportunities on a daily basis. Above all, get rooted and established in *agape*. Work at it - set goals, give time, energy and resources to it. Make it the goal of your life to develop the character of Christ. Be restored into the image of God and, in so doing, you will definitely reconcile people back to God and play a part in restoring them into the image of God.

Remember the following pattern:

We change our hearts.

Renew our minds

Restore our souls.

What stage are you at today?

Even though I had been a Christian for 16 years, including serving God as a pastor and missionary, I realise now that I had not understood this most essential of Christian doctrines, the reality that FAITH EQUALS RIGHTEOUSNESS.

It is not performance that leads to righteousness - it is faith. Oh what a revelation. If you have faith in Christ then despite lapses in your behaviour, you are righteous before God. No wonder we have called this Amazing Grace! This status will get you to heaven, but, in itself, it won't get you a blessed life. That state is down to obedience.

"Abraham believed God and it was credited to him as righteousness" Romans 4:6-8

David says the same thing when he speaks of the blessedness of the man to whom God credits righteousness apart from works. Psalm 32:1-2 says,

*"Blessed are they whose transgressions are forgiven, whose sins are covered. Blessed is the man whose sin the Lord will **never** count against him."*

NEVER! The reason that our sins are not counted against us is because righteousness has been credited to us. If faith equates to righteousness, then how does it equate to the rest of the package of the gospel? Think on this for a moment: if we receive eternity by believing (only), then surely all things are received by believing, that is through faith! Satan is warring against this revelation and, in my case, he had almost won the battle. More than I needed the medical profession (and I did), I needed an injection of faith. There is no doctor on earth who can heal a spiritual problem through medicine alone.

"Now faith is being sure of what we hope for and certain of what we do not see. This is what the ancients were commended for. And without faith it is impossible to please God because anyone who comes to Him must believe that He exists and that He rewards those who earnestly seek Him." Hebrews 11:1 and 11:6

Faith believes the impossible!

Remember that faith is not a product of the reasoning faculties but of the recreated spirit! There are two kinds of knowledge - sense knowledge and revelation knowledge. Since January 2001, I had been forced to find this out. My survival and the welfare of my family depended on it. The issue ceased to be merely a theological topic.

Faith has to believe back before faith can believe forward.

"By faith we understand that the universe was formed at God's command, so that what is seen was not made out of what was visible." Hebrews 11:3

Until we believe this, reason will win the day.

"By faith, he (Abraham) left Egypt, not fearing the king's anger; he persevered because he saw Him who is invisible" Hebrews 11:27

"The only thing that counts is faith expressing itself through agape." Galatians 6:9

You have to believe what God has done in the past before you can believe God for the future. Likewise, there are times when you have to look back to what God has already said to you. Faith is believing not feeling. Faith is seeing the invisible because the word of God declares it to be true. We must look at life through the grid of scripture. There is an amazing place to come to in Him. God asks us to believe back at a personal level as well to what He has said about us. For example:

"Reckon yourself dead to sin..." Romans 6:11

"You died to sin so how can you live in it any longer." Romans 6:7

"Without faith it is impossible to please God." Hebrews 11:6

"This is the work of God to believe in the one who He sent and to agape one another has He commanded us." 1 John 3:23

"You are more than a conqueror." Romans 8:37

I could go on...

Suffice to say we must believe what God has said! I struggled to believe God particularly in relation to what God's word had to say positively about me. This is why I needed to be rooted and established in love at God's level. I needed to see the extent in which God loves me. God makes it clear in His word just how much He *agapes* us and the same is true regarding health and well being. If we don't understand just how much God loves us, then we will be fodder for the enemy because he will always convince us that we are experiencing evil because we have let God down. Be warned because this battle worsens for those who are seeking to be "pure in heart". As I stated previously, sin, law and perceived judgment will come to us hand in hand.

So, if we are to receive healing in the present we must look back to what God has said in the past. We have to focus on universal truth, declared, once and for all, in the past and then remove the present day obstacles that are keeping us from experiencing that universal truth. In this sense the present has already been determined by the past:

"He took up our sickness and our infirmities and by His stripes we are healed." Matthew 8:17

"Abraham believed God and it was credited to him as righteousness." Romans 4:3

Can you begin to see this as a pattern?

If we believe what God says about healing, will healing be credited to us?

It is clear from Scripture that God looks for faith more than moral perfection. The promises of God are activated in our lives when we look at the three things that remain:

"Now these three things remain; faith hope and agape."
1 Corinthians 13:13

We believe and obey God's commands to *agape*. This foundation fills our hearts with hope that we can receive the promises of God by faith. Your confidence lifts immensely when you know that God knows it is your desire and practice to keep the Royal Law found in Scripture.

Faith is something we do. We must reason if you (God) have said this then I will do it. *Agape* is something we do! It is imperative to know that we really must discipline ourselves to both hear and speak the language of faith, which is, in reality, the language of *agape*.

We have a responsibility, an obligation. If you continually want to receive by faith then you must walk in the Spirit. This means you must do whatever is necessary for you to walk in the Spirit.

As this revelation took root in my heart, my confidence began to grow and I started to sleep like a baby. In fact, better than I had ever done. I was still feeling weakness in my heart at times and I went back to Manchester, where I had my operation, for a further consultation. Strangely, as the day approached, the worse I began to feel and as I sat in my Consultant's office, I felt very low. My Consultant entered reading my notes. As he slowly walked through the office, he said, 'Hmm you have been through a pretty difficult time' he murmured and then paused before continuing with something totally unexpected, 'well I won't need to see you again because you are cured.'

I didn't feel cured but I thanked him and left feeling that somehow God had spoken that day. Even though my Consultant was not speaking to me out of a spiritual perspective, I received those words by faith and took them to heart. In the time that has passed since, I'm glad to say I have not needed to see him again. In fact, as I write I am very sportingly active again, jogging, swimming, going to the gym etc. all things I never thought I would do again (it is now over 13 years since that day in my Consultant's office) I have recently completed a seven mile run - the furthest I have run for several years. If we can hear from God and then see it in the spirit, we will

---

eventually do it. In those 13 years, I have not had to take one day off work due to sickness. Wow! One of the secret things I learned during that period of darkness in 2000/2001 was:

The same Spirit that raised Christ from the dead is dwelling in me giving life to my mortal flesh. Romans 8:11

What riches are ahead for those who will learn to walk in the Spirit?

"So I say, live by the Spirit, and you will not gratify the desires of the sinful nature. For the sinful nature desires what is contrary to the Spirit and the Spirit what is contrary to the sinful nature. They are in conflict with each other, so that you do not do what you want. But if you are led by the Spirit, you are not under Law." Galatians 5:16

What does it mean by, *you are not under Law?*

Well the scripture tells us that, *He who agapes his fellow man has fulfilled the Law.* Romans 13:8

This is true because of Jesus' words in Matthew 22:37-40,

"Agape the Lord your God with all your heart, with all your soul and with all your mind. This is the first and greatest commandment. And the second is like it; agape your neighbour as yourself. All the Law and the prophets hang on these two commandments."

Again, we need to stress that this *agape* is no ordinary love, it is *agape* that enters our world from another world. It is nothing less than the character and nature of a God of love flowing from the essence of His being. God has poured this love into our hearts in order that we in turn can pour it out of our hearts. It is love that destroys our enemies by making them our friends, love that would rather be wronged than seek revenge, love that delights to give grace, mercy, forgiveness and possessions even when it is not merited. It is *agape* that does not treat others or us as our sin deserves. It is the first and greatest command and also the greatest need of the church.

Every decision and action should be made from the foundation of this level of love, because, *God is agape*. This love far exceeds all other attempts to love because it is the only level of love that places no conditions. This is how we know what agape is,

"Jesus Christ laid down His life for us and we ought to lay down our lives for our brothers." 1 John 3:16

It is fair to say, wherever God's agape flows, God's presence abides. The Great Commission relies on God's church to live out the great commandment! On from this: we need to understand that it is no use setting goals for the Great Commission if we will not do so out of the foundation of the great commandment.

Most things that we do can be imitated but not this - it is impossible to imitate love at God's intended level and this is surely the point of the command. Jesus himself alluded to the fact that the way we love one another is the ingredient by which men would know that His disciples belonged to Him. This is our greatest evangelistic tool in proving that Jesus is alive.

The decision to walk in this love is far more powerful than receiving a miracle of healing because it will turn an otherwise selfish person into a self-less person. What a witness such a person becomes!

"Agape covers a multitude of sins." 1 Peter 4:8

"Agape never fails." 1 Corinthians 13:8

"Now these three remain, faith, hope and agape."
1 Corinthians 13:13

Behold a great truth; the Great Commission must be fulfilled out of the great command!

How difficult it is for us to understand that God will not accept anything less from us than the fulfilling of His commands to *agape*. Because we have, in the main, offered far less to Him we do not realise what we have denied others and ourselves. It is time to prove life at this level. What will God do in response to our fulfilment of His commands? The answer is more than we can hope, ask or imagine! That is, He will turn up and do all the things that we have been trying to do in our own strength. True maturity is measured by our ability to love unconditionally. This is the revolution that God is seeking - this will turn our communities upside down. It will!

"Do not judge and you will not be judged, do not condemn and you will not be condemned. Forgive and you will be forgiven. Give and it will be given to you. A good measure pressed down, shaken together and running over, will be poured into your lap. For with the measure you use it will be measured to you." Luke 6:37

Often this Scripture is quoted in relation to money but it goes much further than money. It says you will be judged to the same measure that you are condemning others. Are you judging? Are you condemning? If you are don't try and justify it, because it is self-defeating. However, if you have to forgive big sins committed against you, God will forgive you of the big sins that you commit. So do you need to forgive anybody some big sins? If you do, then store up some mercy credit in your own account by going ahead and forgiving.

Don't Judge! Don't Condemn! Do forgive!

It is so clear as to be obvious but, repeatedly, we do not keep God's word and, at worst, we choose to ignore it.

The Apostle Paul said,

"The only thing that counts is faith expressing itself through agape." Galatians 6:9

We have a problem because we all justify our condemnation and judgment of other believers. Forgiveness and acceptance are total in God's economy. The goal of our lives and the stress upon our wills should be that we: *love one another as He has loved us.* I have certainly not lived this out to the degree that the Lord wants me to but I do believe in it with all my heart and, hopefully, I am pressing on toward this.

57

This kind of love is lived out of the will and not the feelings. We are called to do it regardless of how we may feel. Sure, it will be tested but
there is a never-ending fountain of God's grace so that we can indeed find God's strength in the midst of our trials. If you want to forgive, you can forgive because it is a supernatural thing.

"We know that we have passed from death to life because we agape our brothers, anyone who does not agape remains in death." John 3:14

Note again: the level of love that is demanded of us. *Agape* is the greatest power in the universe. At the scene of the crucifixion, it caused an earthquake, people to come out of their graves and an inanimate object to tear. Yet, we are usually so poor at living out this side of the Christian life, that we have no proof of life in this direction. Are we expecting God to move in power when we will not forgive people for far less than God has had to forgive us for?

We owe a debt of love at this level. As we have seen:

"Let no debt remain outstanding except the continuing debt of agape."
Romans 13:8

Listen for the voice of the Lord: *"above all, agape one another."*

Without any shadow of doubt, *agape* equates to power! At any moment we are only a decision away from this kind of love. Our general inability to understand this subject has cost us more than we can imagine. For me, it has been a personal journey over many years.

As I took up pastoral ministry again in Porth, I was determined to lay a new foundation. After all, I had suffered this lack of unconditional love in Porth, seen others suffer and, no doubt, made others suffer. The same can be said of my time in Africa and would, of course, be repeated in any situation. This time I had come amongst a hurting people. I continued to speak of *agape* in practically every sermon and gradually one by one I could sense that people were being healed in their hearts. God is true to His word!

As I write this part of the book, I am overlooking the beautiful afore mentioned, Oxwich Bay on South Wales' Gower Peninsular.

I have had an interesting day attending an evangelism seminar with the Elim church. Later I called in at the Bible College of Wales, the place built, by faith, by Rhys Howells. It was good to breathe in the atmosphere of the college and all that it has stood for over the years. Like many of the great and renowned evangelical sites that survive in Wales, without God's hand in the present day, it was in danger of becoming a museum piece. Thankfully, I'm glad to say, in more recent times, the college has found renewed purpose due to a spiritual and financial investment from overseas.

Later, I walked through the village of Oxwich and I saw a plaque on a cottage proclaiming that John Wesley had stayed there and preached five times from there over the years. I imagined this legend of a man travelling for hours on horseback to what must have seemed such a remote place to him to deposit the gospel in the hearts of his listeners. What a heritage! One is reminded of the tremendous role that Christianity has played in forming all that is great in Wales. Why then is Wales and the British nation at large so indifferent today? What would have happened if the teaching of the Royal Law had been paramount rather than the oft-mentioned bigotry and pride that overwhelmed the populace, particularly since the great Welsh revival in 1904?

The revival began in Moriah chapel, Loughor and it is still revered throughout the evangelical world and remains a place of pilgrimage for many. Nevertheless, many of the inhabitants of Loughor today have no idea where Moriah chapel is, let alone it's significance.

I gave this prophecy in 1995 during an Evangelistic crusade with Marilyn Harry in Ynyshir, Rhondda.

'God will not revive His church in Wales if we remain apathetic and if we will not pursue holiness. Revival will remain but a dream if we will not allow God into our comfort zones to stir us up and cause us

to will revival. We must realise that, by and large, we have moved far from real Biblical Christianity. God is calling us back to the simplicity of a pursuit of holy living and a willingness to obey Him no matter what the cost. God is taking us out of our comfort zones and into the adventure of action packed, risk taking, obedience to His voice. We must adopt God-centred living and build churches that reflect God rather than having people at the centre of their function and mandates. In this day of reckoning will anyone pay the price that will bring revival? Can God gather enough sufficiently dead-to-self people to fill the pulpits of our land, so that His voice can truly speak and not be watered down? Can enough people be gathered to forsake all in order to impact Wales at a national level? Will enough gather to share the burden, weep the tears and pray the prayers to reverse our fall from grace? The word of the Lord is: Set the trumpet to your mouths, hearken and speak my words rather than platitudes of what peoples' itching ears want to hear. Speak my words! Speak my words! For my words will surely be accompanied by my power.'

I also gave the following prophetic word in Porth in 2001

'Set the trumpet to your mouth and call back all the wounded and defeated sheep, for I will turn them into an army that will sweep this land. Many are waiting to hear that they have another chance and my grace is sufficient; many of these sheep have been abused through leadership and hurt by my body which has acted through lack of knowledge and lack of wisdom.'

I believe that I should acknowledge that we have not kept the Royal Law as we should have and I believe that we follow that acknowledgement by repenting. If we do, we can then set about creating a new norm that will be in place for future generations. The enemy has outsmarted us because we closed the door marked, 'Royal Law.'

Maybe due to this we have faced needless death in the truest sense of the word. In the Bible, the word 'death,' never means cessation of life – it always means separation. To be disconnected from God is spiritual death. Physical death is separation from the body. All new life comes through death, burial and resurrection. If I can know Him in the power of His suffering, I can know Him in His resurrection. Expect to face some little deaths. You are perpetually going through a cycle of death, burial and resurrection - that is normal Christian living - but what you thought would happen, during the death period, hasn't. Jesus is always on time!

Remember the grain of wheat principle. In Christianity, death leads to multiplication. Normal activity leads to addition but it is death that leads to multiplication. Death is separation! Listen, death is separation! That is why there are times when you will not feel God's presence. But you must have the following attitude, 'I'm coming up out of it'.

"No weapon forged against you will prevail." Isaiah 54:17

When the veil, in the temple, was torn from top to bottom on the day of Jesus' Resurrection, God was demonstrating more than just His power – He was demonstrating His intent. Jesus saw the heavens tear. If necessary, God will tear up heaven to get you out of the problem you are facing. The answer is written in the sky!

During our visit back to the UK, before my illness, I was preaching in Treorchy in the Rhondda Valleys. On the afternoon preceding the evening meeting I was praying with a friend when I felt God say, 'The answer is written in the sky'. At the time that I said those words, I had no idea what it meant or of the relevance that it would have upon my faith.

One day after my return to the Rhondda, I felt God ask me, what did I think was beyond the stars. Quite by chance I did a bit of amateur astronomy. There is so much out there beyond what we can see, even with a telescope, but heaven must be torn in order for you to see it.

The Bible says, *"He who descended has also ascended to fill the whole universe."* Ephesians 4:10

We must pray in authority, at the same time as keeping the Royal Law, until we create an open heaven because when the heavens are torn open we shall see a mirror image of the life of God as it should be lived and worked out in His presence. Death is a wonderful thing if you deal with it properly! It is merely a temporal separation from what you have known.

We are not too perturbed if we are out-sung by the crowds in the rock world; not too dismayed if we are out-given by the charities; not too downhearted if our building projects are not recognised but we should be absolutely tortured if we are out-loved by any group on this earth. God is *agape*!

It is not enough to recognise God through the miraculous acts we perform – other people can perform miraculous acts. We will only truly be recognised by the extent of our love!

We cannot interpret the things surrounding God, His church and His people through natural means. Most believers who are not spiritually aware do just that. The first question that we need to ask is, what is God doing in this, and secondly, what will be achieved for God in this?

The question of authority has been settled once and for all – God won and Satan lost. The problem is we have ignored God's blue print on how to affect the victory. Oh how blind we have been – we would rather shout at a dodging target than love our neighbour.

If only we can grasp the amount of grace that has been apportioned to us and then respond to others with the same levels of grace, we would begin to move mountains.

CHAPTER 6
BY THE WAY OF THE CROSS

"For the message of the cross is foolishness to those who are perishing, but to us who are being saved it is the power of God."
1 Corinthians 1:18

So often our natural response to revelation of the true gospel according to God's amazing grace is: 'this is too good to be true'.

"What shall we say then? Shall we go on sinning so that grace may increase? By no means! We died to sin; how can we live in it any longer? Or don't you know that all of us who were baptised into Christ Jesus were baptised into His death? We were therefore buried with Him through baptism into death in order that, just as Christ was raised from the dead through the glory of the Father, we too may live a new life. If we have been united with Him like this in His death we will certainly also be united with Him in His resurrection. For we know that our old self was crucified with Him so that the body of sin might be done away with, that we should no longer be slaves to sin – because anyone who has died has been freed from sin." Romans 6:6-8

If you truly come by way of the cross, then you have been crucified with Christ and you no longer live but Christ lives in you. This has happened – past tense. (See my book, 'How to Live so you'll never have to die' for a better understanding on what the Bible means by death.)

You do not have to keep crucifying yourself. In fact you can't, you simply have to reckon yourself dead or realise that it has happened, past tense, once and for all. The battle in the mind goes like this: 'how can you be crucified when you still think that way and still do the sinning that you do?' I shall seek to answer this.

You have been crucified and you have been resurrected. This has already taken place. The fact that you are still very much alive does not negate the fact that you have died.

I used to think that when the Apostle Paul wrote, *"I have been crucified with Christ and I no longer live but Christ lives in me, the life I live in the body I live by faith in the Son of God who died and gave Himself for me"* (Galatians 2:22), that he had achieved something that few believers achieve.

One day, however, God revealed to me that this is the state of all born again believers. We just don't realise it or reckon it to be true.

"Now, if we died with Christ, we believe that we will also live with Him. For we know that since Christ was raised from the dead, He cannot die again; death no longer has mastery over Him. The death He died He died to sin once for all; but the life He lives, He lives to God. In the same way, count (reckon) yourselves dead to sin but alive to God in Christ Jesus. Therefore do not let sin reign in your mortal body so that you obey its evil desires. Do not offer the parts of your body to sin, as instruments of wickedness, but rather offer yourselves to God, as those who have been brought from death to life; and offer the parts of your body to Him as instruments of righteousness. For sin shall not be your master because you are not under law but under grace." Romans 6:8-14

"Reckon yourself dead to sin but alive to God in Christ Jesus."

Don't stand at the crossroads; decide to be a kingdom person. Don't waver any longer at the crossroads of indecision, 'reckon!'

The Kingdom of God bares absolutely no resemblance to this world. None at all! We live in a parallel universe. One part is fuelled by sense knowledge; one is fuelled by revelation knowledge. In and through us, the one should bring the other into submission. The Spirit is superior. Once we realise this then we will run to God, we will hunger and thirst after God. We will do anything to bring heaven's blessing into the earth's atmosphere.

Sense knowledge is governed by seeing. Revelation knowledge is governed by hearing. Some of us can't hear because we are dominated by what we see. People can become a blockage because God sees what they will be whereby we see only what they are or perversely what they are not! Stop letting your faith be dominated by sight and start letting it be dominated by what you hear.

Listen and hear: *"Faith comes by hearing and hearing by the word of God."* Romans 10:17

Because we have not yet seen, we struggle to believe what we have heard. But we are working to God's time scale and not Him to ours. We often disqualify ourselves because we lift revelation from the heart and store it in the mind. We move from revelation knowledge and rely again on sense knowledge.

"So we live by faith and not by sight." 2 Corinthians 5:7

"We fix our eyes not on what is seen but what is unseen for what is seen is temporary but what is unseen is eternal." 2 Corinthians 4:18

Faith comes by hearing, because the hearing takes you beyond your seen horizons. You have subconsciously imposed boundaries, barriers and limitations on your life.

Undo the lie today and begin to hear what the Bible says about you. Then take the step of faith through the doorway and into life in the kingdom of God.

As we have seen, in simple terms, the kingdom of God has clauses written into it, God says, 'If you will do this then I will do that.'

Often, we have to unlearn the way that we have learned in the past. Come out of your prison and begin to live at God's level. Live a parallel life. Live by kingdom principles! We must stop seeing this as a negative – it is absolutely positive.

Would you rather be nobody and gain the benefits of the Kingdom or be somebody in the eyes of the world and not gain the benefits of the Kingdom. That is, all God promises in the present and eternity beyond that.

As we have seen, sin and Law walk toward you hand in hand – the sin to trap you, the law to make you feel condemned. This is swiftly followed by deceitful judgment, the devil's attempt to convince you of a lie concerning your future. So God says the Law is no longer in effect in the life of the believer. It is once and for all abolished because it has fully served its purpose in evangelising you. Can you see it? Many have believed a lie, a lie that tells us that God expected us to keep the Law. Learn today God does not expect you to keep the Mosaic Law. He expects you to keep the Royal Law of love.

Marvel at the following Scriptures:

"All who rely on observing the Law are under a curse, for it is written, 'Cursed is everyone who does not continue to do everything written in the book of the Law.' Clearly no-one is justified before God by the Law, because The Righteous will live by faith. The Law is not based on faith; on the contrary, the man who does these things will live by them. Christ redeemed us from the curse of the Law by becoming a curse for us, for it is written, "Cursed is everyone who is hanged on a tree". He redeemed us in order that the blessing given to Abraham might come to the Gentiles through faith in Christ Jesus, so that by faith we might receive the promise of the Spirit." Galatians 3:10-14

"What then was the purpose of the Law? It was added because of transgressions until the seed to whom the promise referred had come." V19

The Law is not for the believer, grace is for the believer. Can you receive that into your spirit right now? It is true. Don't be shortsighted because it will keep you from seeing the things that you are hearing about beyond your horizon. The hearing will always take you beyond the seeing if you act on it.

I remember the time when I saw a programme that revealed the secrets of street magicians. When you see how they do their 'magic' you cease to ask 'How do they do that?' There is no wonder or amazement because every trick is simply an illusion. The simplicity of which often leaves one feeling amazed. It is difficult to believe that something that can hold the uninitiated spellbound can be created so simply, what a con!

The more experience I gain on this planet, the more I think that nothing is as it seems. So much of what appears is a con. Take people, how much of the real person is usually hidden behind the image of what we see and thus perceive.

Another lesson that I learned recently was that of perspective. It was the story of a blind man who underwent an operation that resulted in him seeing only to tragically lose his sight again. However, the true story dealt with the fact that though the man could now physically see, his brain held no perspective of what he was now seeing. This is really quite obvious but not something I had ever considered! Surely it is a different matter interpreting an object through its texture if you have previously seen it than it is if you have not previously seen it. But coordination between sight and texture cannot exist if a person has touched something before he has seen it. I was told in Africa that the average African has no concept of a good view or vista. But what is a good view? What is for you may not be for me.

Left to his own devices, man will perceive reality whereas God reveals reality. Long before the relative normalisation of such things, as young sailors we would come across seemingly beautiful women who were really men. Don't be taken in by what you see, it may well be just an illusion. This is why many people think they have fallen in love when in reality they have gained an infatuation!

I wonder if this is why God ordained that faith should come by hearing and not by seeing. What we see is really open to interpretation, or levels of physical capabilities, e.g. can a person with cataracts see the same shades as a fully sighted person? And at a spiritual level, what about seeing the faults of a person to the degree that you can no longer hear what God is saying through that person.

I wonder also if this is why people hear the Lord proportionately much more than people see Him. I mean, is Jesus Black, Yellow, White or something in between? Faith comes by hearing and hearing by the word of God. The Lord jealously guards the Word – detract from it at your peril – and surely it is so dependable because of its unchanging nature.

The eyes of the heart are meant to interpret what we see. When I first lived in Tanzania I learned to buy things due to the person's worth rather than the worth of the goods. Maybe I had learned to see the vendors through the eyes of my heart. The apostle Paul said,

"I pray that the eyes of your heart maybe opened that you may know..." Ephesians 1:18

Is this why the devil seeks to harden the hearts of believers and unbelievers by causing us to harbour grievance or hold offence in our hearts. He is formidable at it; that is why Jesus had to command us to *agape,* 'Father do not hold this sin against them.' Don't allow what you are seeing to interpret either God or people, for this is not God's way. Reality comes through the Word, which transcends human experience to the point that it delivers God's thoughts and ways into the heart of man.

Do you often have cause to exclaim: 'I've seen it all before!' Truth is, we all do because we all have, to some degree. As someone once rightly said, 'what we see is determined by what we are looking out from'. And as the heart is the wellspring of life, we do well not to clog it up. Raise your gaze above the haze and see that the sun is always shining above the clouds.

I guarantee if you allow God to open the eyes of your heart you will see both situations and people differently, including, importantly, yourself. This is vital because when you see your position in Christ you will know that this will always overcome your condition in the world, if you apply the Word of God to your condition! If you take heed of what you hear from God you will begin to see in direct proportion to your readiness to hear and obey. We may well sit side by side in the same church week after week but

I have learned that we are definitely not all seeing the same things. As long as a person can hear from God he will eventually see.

What do people really see in you? I wonder if any of us are truly aware? Have you ever wondered what people repeatedly mention as you leave the scene?

Grace and truth go hand in hand but truth is much more difficult to receive than grace is.

Oh the wonder that we are no longer under the Law. It has served its intended purpose in your life by evangelising you because Jesus didn't come into the world to condemn it but rather through Him the world might be saved. You are under grace my friend. Realise it, rejoice in it and live accordingly. Heaven is prepared to receive you and it lasts forever. God will lay the red carpet out for you, yes, you! If you are born again you have already, wonderfully, gained eternal life. Now move on, in this life, until you are mature and complete not lacking anything.

Put aside your own perspective because no doubt it has led to illusions and begin to see yourself from God's perspective. You are His child and when you fully realise this you will begin to treat others with the same level of *agape* and grace that you have received. You are indeed standing under the canopy of amazing grace!

"What then? Shall we sin because we are not under the law but under grace? By no means! Don't you know that when you offer yourselves to someone to obey him as slaves, you are slaves to the one whom you obey – whether you are slaves to sin, which leads to death, or to obedience, which leads to righteousness? But thanks be to God that, though you used to be slaves to sin, you wholeheartedly obeyed the form of teaching to which you were entrusted. You have been set free from sin and have become slaves to righteousness. I put this in human terms because you are weak in your natural selves. Just as you used to offer the parts of your body in slavery to impurity and to ever-increasing wickedness, so now offer them in slavery to righteousness leading to holiness. When you were slaves to sin, you were free from the control of righteousness. What benefit did you

reap at that time from the things that you are now ashamed of? Those things result in death! But now that you have been set free from sin and have become slaves to God, the benefit you reap leads to holiness, and the result is eternal life. For the wages of sin is death, but the gift of God is eternal life in Christ Jesus, our Lord." Romans 6:15-23,

We are to live in God's grace by serving Him unconditionally.

"The least in the Kingdom of God is greater than John the Baptist." Matthew 11:11

Can we see that? Really see it. Once we see it then everything will change.

You see, to be least in the Kingdom of God is to have infinitely more than the richest, most successful person who is not in the Kingdom of God. If we can, for a moment, understand heaven economically (whether or not there will be money in heaven I don't know) even if you only earn a pound a year in eternity it will accumulate to far more than Bill Gates could earn in a lifetime on earth.

Think about it. If you only save one pound a year in heaven – if you save it for a billion years you will become a billionaire and still have eternity to spend it.

'Now let the poor say I am rich'

Listen regularly to the language of faith because your mind is not neutral.

The deal is this – God asks us to submit to Him now to the degree that He can live out His purpose through us. In simple terms, the gospel is as follows: we give Him our hearts now and He gives us all heaven in the future in addition to all the things that we need now.

You cannot live the Christian life on your own, your only hope is to submit to the one who can and you submit to Christ by walking in the Spirit, thus allowing Him to live His life through you. Hear me,

70

whoever you are, no matter what you have achieved at a human level, no matter how long you have been a Christian, you cannot live the Christian life – you can merely submit to the one who can.

Once we realise that in order to be great in the Kingdom, we have to be prepared to be nobody in the world (that is according to how the world sees it), then we'll place ourselves at His feet. We will allow nothing to stop us from gaining His favour. A hard pill to swallow because we must take it in faith that what God says is true is, in fact, true.

The Kingdom of God is a Kingdom of grace, mercy, humility and *agape*. These are some of the attributes that bring your personal greatness and success in the Kingdom of God. The more you will humble yourself, the greater you will become. The more truth you accept, the more truth you will see. The more you are prepared to love at the *agape* level, the more power you will receive.

We must come by way of the cross. The cross means death before it means resurrection, but, every death in Christ is followed by a resurrection and this resurrection leads to multiplication. The problem we face is our reluctance to accept death. You have died but unless you understand this, you will never learn to walk in resurrection life.

We have an awful scene in the church today whereby people are seeking to gain the anointing through earthly means, through talent and strong personality but these are not the ingredients that gain the anointing. The anointing is gained through the condition of the heart. The heart begets true talent and the heart begets anointing.

Often, success in the world comes at the expense of the heart. So when the heart is tested we often fall back on the old nature and fail the test.

How blind we have been!

It is one thing being born again but it is entirely another thing to live life in the kingdom.

"For me to live is Christ, to die is gain." Philippians 1:21

Don't speak the language of your emotions. And don't speak the language of defeat – neither belongs in the eternal Kingdom of God. Doubt breeds doubt. Hear me again: the Kingdom that you enter now is an eternal Kingdom. Things are being worked out according to an eternal perspective.

You are, *more than a conqueror* when you feel like it and you are still *more than a conqueror* when you don't feel like it. You have conquered death because, in Christ, you have died already and been resurrected. Conviction still has a great role in your life but conviction is not condemnation – even though they may feel the same.

You are convicted when you are under grace and condemned when you are under the Law. As you are not under Law, your days of being condemned are over even though you are imperfect and are continuing to behave, at times, in a way that you are ashamed of. God is big enough to handle this – He is always good and Satan is always bad!

Jesus is the way, He is the truth and, therefore, He is the life.

Look beyond the sky and see a spiritual world that is beyond the ability of our senses to interpret. It is the parent world. It was here before the creation of matter. God is calling us to live back in the SUPERIOR and the devil hates it! Break the chains and walk free.

This is why when the word of God is sown as seed, the devil wants to steal the seed before it has had a chance to germinate and produce the immense potential that is contained in the seed.

We have a new day. You have a new day if you'll take it. Stop hearing God and dismissing it because of what you see. Wherever you live and whatever church you belong to, what you see will always get in the way of what you hear!

"Faith comes by hearing". By hearing and NOT BY SEEING! God knows that you will always interpret life by what you see. So

72

He determined not to limit our expectations of Him by what we see but rather we could go further by what we hear and believe. We have to move from hearing to listening and from listening to doing, and then we can move on to the next level. If you hear and obey, God will open the eyes of your heart so that you can see!

So if God says, *He took up our sickness and our infirmities.* It is not enough to disprove this just because you haven't seen it. Faith will not submit to scientific analysis or the traditions and expectancy of man because faith is superior to scientific analysis and the rest.

True preaching is not telling about God, it is saying what God is saying.

We don't believe because the previous generation didn't believe and they didn't believe because the generation before them didn't believe. Somebody has got to start believing. Preaching fell under the influence of this world and became a matter of pride and eloquence rather than the 'telling forth from God'.

How fickle we can be. We say 'preach it brother' until what is being preached affects us! Then there is a strange silence. That's why any preacher worth his weight will take platitudes from man with a pinch of salt.

The Bible was inspired by the Holy Spirit and written by scribes thousands of years ago but is still living today.

Faith comes by hearing because some of us can't see beyond today.

Don't miss out on what he is saying because of what you are seeing!

If you see it, it's not permanent.

"But my righteous one will live by faith and if he shrinks back I will not be pleased by him." Hebrews 10:38

"For in the gospel a righteousness from God is revealed, a righteousness that is by faith from first to last just as it is written: the righteous will live by faith." Romans 1:17

Do we believe we are just? Being 'just' is a reflection on our status as children of God. This status is a gift.

Those who know they are just no longer have to justify themselves. The just believe what God says about them not what people think. We have so much but there are barriers to what we are receiving. Faith must go beyond what we see. We come through and into. You will only live in the power of the new to the degree that you will let go of the old. Come on now! Come to the cross and reckon. Realise these following words:

"If any man be in Christ Jesus he is a new creation, the old has gone, behold all things are new." 2 Corinthians 5:17

You have to believe that what took place at Calvary, as it pertains to you when you come to the cross, actually took place. The Apostle Paul was not the only one who has been crucified with Christ. You have been crucified with Christ and so have I. The difference is in realisation. Once you realise it, you have begun the process of living accordingly. The old has gone so don't resurrect it! Walk away from your past and into the provision of your future in God. You have a choice, live in the old even though it has been crucified or actively put off the old and live in the new. Your strength in God will be in direct proportion to the condition of your heart. Sin has been dealt with vicariously. It was God who initiated it and completed it Himself without our help or even our concession. Self is a different matter.

The fact that your sins have been dealt with, has given you access into the Kingdom of God – the parallel Kingdom. Access into it does not guarantee that you will live successfully in it. Self is now your problem.

The missionary Jim Elliot said 'live in such a way that when it's time to die, all that you have to do is die.'

Adopt the following attitude towards all people, 'I disagree with what you do but not with you.' Recognise the times when God comes to test you and don't side with Satan by allowing your Christian walk to lose its passion.

"You were taught, with regard to your former life, to put off your old self, which is being corrupted by its deceitful desires; to be made new in the attitude of your minds; and to put on the new self, created to be like God in true righteousness and holiness." Ephesians 4:22-24

Put off the old instead of allowing it to live side by side with the new. It cannot co-exist. There is a bridge from the old over to the new and that bridge is to be found in v23

"To be made new in the attitude of your minds"

So don't feed your old self – there are some things that the new self will refuse to be fed on. Therefore, the old has no place in feeding the new. It will only succeed in nourishing and adding strength to the pull of the old man. In order for the new self to grow and mature, we must find out what nourishes it.

Originally man was made in the image of God. At the fall the image was lost. But when we are saved, the new self is created to be like God in true righteousness and holiness. Righteousness has been credited to you but holiness has not. Holiness happens as we are restored into the image of God. This means we become like Him in character. This is not beyond us – it is what God expects from all of us because that is where the true benefits of our adoption are realised.

Get the beginning point and, in the future, you will find that what you have prayed then is happening now. I am experiencing that now as I hear God with regard to our future in Tanzania. What we prayed back in 1999 is happening now; what we confessed then is happening now. There are reasons why God answers prayers and responds to confessions of faith and there are reasons why He does not. Do what is necessary to find out why God answers prayer. It is not worth holding on to the past – deal with it ruthlessly. This means we will have to change our lifestyle in order to put off so that we can 'cross the bridge', to be made new in the attitude of our minds; before we can put on the new self created to be like God. The crossing of the bridge will not be in the conventional manner.

We cannot see what is beyond the bridge but we can hear about it and pursue it. In fact the bridge does not really exist. It is a figment of the mind of the natural man. God does not use conventional bridges; He uses more spiritual means. Hear and follow! When I was looking to God to answer the intricate questions surrounding my situation all I could hear was: trust, follow and obey. It was enough.

At any given time, the following is true; we have not yet become all that we are. This is true of you and it is true of me. There is a practical solution. Having realised our present condition we must obey the following injunction:

"Do not offer the parts of your body to sin, as instruments of wickedness, but rather offer yourselves to God, as those who have been brought from death to life; and offer the parts of your body to Him as instruments of righteousness. For sin shall not be your master, because you are not under law, but under grace." Romans 6:13-14

Sin is not a good paymaster but you must fill your life with righteousness or you will slide into its web – guaranteed! Let me repeat something vital here. If you are a Christian, you must realise that you are no longer under Law but under grace. The reason for this is clear, has been stated but is worth repeating: Law has served its purpose in evangelising you i.e. making you conscious of your need of a Saviour. Allow the grace you now stand in to launch you into realising your potential. It is time to put self on the line and sign the consent form so that God can help you put off in order to put on.

If you are still anchored in the old self, you will have to put up with the dominion that the old self lived in but there is something infinitely better. Realise that self must die so that you can begin to live the eternal now! It is not as difficult as you may imagine.

CHAPTER 7
DELIVER US FROM EVIL

"Then the dragon was enraged at the woman and went off to wage war against the rest of her offspring – those who keep God's commands and hold fast their testimony about Jesus."
Revelation 12:17

As we are putting off in order to put on, we will realise that we have opposition to this that is beyond the obvious, natural opposition.

Everything that we will ever need was obtained for us at Calvary. The potential for you to find healing and deliverance is already in place. It is a case of finding it in God. Do you walk daily in the realisation that you, being in Christ, have authority over all the power of the evil one? Read on and understand...

Here is a clue, *No good thing does He withhold from those whose walk is blameless.* Psalm 84:11

We have an enemy who does not want us to receive all that is rightly ours "In Christ".

This book is really about foundations and the reason for it is this, in order to receive the abundant life that God has promised, we must not be deceived about the necessary foundations. The ingredient by which we now live as children of God is faith and, as we have just seen, faith does not come by seeing it comes by hearing and hearing by the Word of God. So, as we have seen, our future is dependent on what we hear (from God) and not by what we see around us. This is the greater reality that we are seeking.

What we see then has passed through our hearts. So the Apostle Paul prayed,

"I pray that God would open the eyes of your hearts so that you may see." Ephesians 1:18

In the kingdom, hearing only becomes seeing when we pass what we hear from God through the eyes of hearts that are loving God and man at God's intended level. This is another dimension.

The eyes of the heart open up another dimension - the eyes in our head will never see this. We are to look at the world around us and the people around us through the eyes of our hearts. What we are looking out from determines what we see. We have an enemy and we need to understand his tactics. Rather than being a mere personification of evil, there can be no doubt that Satan is revealed to us in Scripture as a created, intelligent being.

So, the Lord's Prayer teaches us to pray,

"Deliver us from the evil one." Matthew 6:13

We are asking the Lord to free us from the effects of an intelligent adversary who is set against us.

The meaning of his name, gives us tremendous insight into his nature.

1. "Satan" means adversary or opposer.
2. "Devil" means slanderer.
3. "The Evil One" denotes the essence of his character.
4. "The Serpent" indicates his guile and craftiness.

One of Satan's activities is to be the accuser of the brethren. He does this unceasingly and he has a good case against us because we do sin. However, the death of Jesus covered our sin – big and small – because sin is a condition and Jesus' death cleansed us from the affect of the condition.

Therefore, we are defended on the sole basis that all our sins were paid for by Christ's death when He paid for SIN!

During my dark night of the soul, I understood the above in theory but I had not made it my own. I was hearing a demonic voice but he was imitating the voice of the Lord. The voice would constantly tell me the worst – it would convince me of horrendous things that were coming my way and that I deserved them. Finally, the voice swore at me and I knew at once that the Lord would not swear. You must realise that I was sleepless and my mind was foggy and depressed.

Satan is also the tempter. He tempted Eve, he tempted Jesus and he tempts all believers, particularly into immorality. (See 1 Corinthians 7:5)

Satan is described as, *"the ruler of this world."* 2 Corinthians 4:4

He is, *"the prince of the power of the air."* Ephesians 2:2

"The whole world is under his control." 1 John 5:19

"He deceives the whole world." Revelation 12:9

"He resides in the air (the heavenly places)." Ephesians 6:12

He is ruler of the cosmos for the duration of this age.

Ryrie said, 'the cosmos is that organised framework of things in which mankind lives and moves and which opposes God by eliminating Him and counterfeiting Him.'

It is a world system headed up by Satan that lives independently of God.

That kind of rule is fearsome apart from the fact that:

"Greater is He that is in us than he that is in the world."

1 John 4:4

In summary of Satan:

Background: accuser, adversary, tempter

Looks: serpent, dragon.

Characteristics: liar, murderer, ruler.

Activities: accuses, tempts, destroys.

This powerful, intelligent being must not be underestimated.

The nature of Satan's sin is reflected to us in 1Timothy 3:6 with regard to the choosing of elders or leaders,

"He must not be a recent convert, or he may become conceited and fall under the same judgment as the devil."

His sin was arrogance, conceit, being puffed up. Not far removed from the sin a new believer might have when he is pushed forward or asserts himself too quickly and begins to take the glory that is God's alone. This is why the commands to *agape* cover all types of sin. The way to unlock the promises of God is to find the keys of humility, grace, mercy, and *agape* – in short to walk in the fruit of the spirit.

"Submit yourselves then to God. Resist the devil and he will flee from you." James 4:7

If you perceive that you are under attack then the first thing to do is not to attack Satan but to submit to God. Learn to enquire of God, 'what is Satan doing concerning me?' Your heavenly Father will not withhold such information from you.

The various names attributed to Satan ought to tell us that he can attack us in various ways, using diverse tactics. The essence of Satan's activity against God is to offer a rival kingdom and programme. This battle is being fought in the mind of mankind in every nation on our planet.

Three general areas that you might be under attack:

1. Conforming to the pressures and structure of society.
2. Being tempted to cover up selfish actions.
3. Being tempted into immorality.

Remember that sin and Law walk hand in hand and lead us towards a wrong perception of judgment. As we have seen, Satan is, *the accuser of the brethren.* His aim is to nullify our witness of the gospel by quenching our understanding of eternal grace. That is why it is imperative that we are rooted and grounded in *agape.*

Firstly, he seeks to turn governmental authority against us. He will imprison or even kill believers. He creates an atmosphere of fear, to the point that we will hide what we are.

Secondly, Satan spotlights our sins. Notice I said sins and not sin. I re-emphasise so that you will realise that your sins were massed into the condition of sin and that is what Jesus died for. He died for sin so that you could be saved from your sins. Your sins (plural) were incorporated into the sin (singular) at the cross when Christ became sin.

How I needed to know that because our enemy will get us to concentrate on the sins that we have personally committed, even convincing you that some were so bad that God couldn't possibly forgive you. Jesus didn't simply die for your sin; He died for sin! He covered every sin ever committed by every person - such was the atonement carried out by Jesus. Allow that truth to help you – it is mind blowing and will convince you that you have not committed the unpardonable sin, that is, if you think you may have.

"If you confess your sin to the Lord (any sin) He is faithful and just to forgive you of your sin and to cleanse you from all unrighteousness."
1 John 1:9

I need to add in response to the above as I write this, a very personal 'Praise the Lord!'

Our understanding of this is one of the greatest battles we need to win. I say again to you child of God, you need to listen to the language of faith and learn to speak it. This will have a remarkable affect on your life. God has brought you out of the kingdom of darkness and into His wonderful light. He did not and has not made a mistake. Are you experiencing the benefits of the light or are you still ensnared by the deceit of the darkness?

Why be a pauper when you can be a joint heir with Christ? This is not a rhetorical question. Take time to ponder it and seek to answer it.

CHAPTER EIGHT
UNDERSTANDING THE COSMOS

"Do not love the world or anything in the world. If anyone loves the world, love for the Father is not in them." 1 John 2:15

The word, translated love here, is *agape*. Don't love this world with the highest form of love that places anything in it above God.

The cosmos (world) has several meanings, but generally, in the New Testament, it is used to describe, this world, as it is set apart from God and functioning according to its own light and reason.

It is the ordered whole completely separate from God.

Ryrie says of the cosmos:

'The cosmos (world) is that system organised by Satan and run by Satan, which leaves God out and is rival to him.'

There is a counterfeit order on our planet headed up by Satan. If we could see the degree that we are all pawns in this system and the way it is linked to world politics, we would all gladly and hurriedly submit ourselves to the Kingdom of God. The inherent evil of the cosmos is not that it is out and out darkness (it contains good things as well as bad) but rather that it is completely independent of the creator God!

In James 4:4 we are told that friendship with the world (cosmos) is hostility toward God.

"All that is in the world is not from the Father." 1 John 2:16

The main pull and attractiveness of the cosmos is that it seeks to place self as number one and the here and now as the most important.

"Do not love (agape) the world or anything in the world; if anyone loves the world, the love of the Father is not in him. For everything in the world, the cravings of sinful man, the lust of his eyes and the

---

boasting of what he has and does comes not from the Father but from the cosmos (world). 1 John 2:15-16

Satan is at work in tempting us to seek satisfaction as our top priority.

Know this, Satan urges us to satisfy the lusts of the flesh by trying to get what our eyes make us desire and covet and then to build a self-sufficient pride and arrogance by boasting about what your lust of the flesh has gained for you. This is the prevailing philosophy of our world and it has no place in the church (the Kingdom of God).

So, we have understood that Satan seeks to divert our thinking by getting us to place self first and the here and now (the temporary) as the most important. Whereby, the gospel teaches that God is first and that eternity is most important. God knows that our thinking needs to change to the degree that our automatic response becomes a Godly one.

The word of the Lord stands forever.

God has already passed sentence on the cosmos; it will be judged and terminated.

The Kingdom of God offers us a different system to live by - The Royal Law. The Royal Law is meant to gird us up and to open a door into the supernatural. It provides all that we need in a world that is diametrically opposed to the children of God, a world that gravitates in the opposite direction.

One dramatic failing in the body of Christ is that we have not seen the absolute imperative of having the Royal Law in place before we seek to operate the gifts of the Spirit. So what we have seen, in the main, is an insipid and ineffective usage of the gifts that can often be governed by 1 John 2:16 rather than the fruit of the Spirit.

"For everything in the world—the lust of the flesh, the lust of the eyes, and the pride of life—comes not from the Father but from the world."

Life in the Kingdom has unparalleled benefits but only if you live by the principles of the Kingdom. God asks us to make our choices!

The fruit and gifts that are available in the Kingdom are sufficient for the total care of its inhabitants. Christ likeness in this cosmos means separation from this cosmos. We cannot *agape* anything in this world for to do so means we place it above our devotion to God. We should do all things as well as and not instead of our devotion to God. Separation is not isolation but it is separation. Our service being devotion to God must not live alongside our old values but rather replace them. The full benefits of the Kingdom will only be realised as we learn to do this. And the full benefits are magnificent.

God wants us to act in such a way that it will cause others to observe our testimony and draw attention to God and, ultimately bring glory to Him.

Become an untouchable by living within the confines of the Kingdom. Obviously, this has no geographical bearing but rather a challenge to how we behave. We should behave in such a way that we live beyond the reaches of the tentacles of the evil one. Don't make a truce with the devil and end up at the negotiating table. His aim is to get you to accept far less than Jesus died to give you. Live in such a way that you implement Christ's total victory. Don't give the enemy a day off concerning your life, live in such a way that you can hound him continuously. Seek a constant connection to your source of life.

Living in the Kingdom of God is a matter of choice.

It is no use living in this cosmos to the degree that we can't take authority over its ruler. When you move into another kingdom you have to adapt to its differences - you can no longer live with some of the principles and traditions of the old kingdom. People are held by illusions. These illusions are created by this world (cosmos) and they create perceptions of reality, whereby, the Scriptures give us a revelation of reality.

The Royal Law is THE foundation of the Kingdom.

"So in everything, do to others what you would have them do to you, for this sums up the Law and the Prophets." Matthew 7:12

Having the capabilities to fulfill the above comes through the baptism in the Holy Spirit. This baptism is the empowering of the kingdom.

"You will receive power when the Holy Spirit comes on you." Acts 1:8

The Gifts of the Holy Spirit are the on-going, supernatural provision of the kingdom. We have been crucified with Christ and baptised into his resurrection. We have been empowered by the baptism in the Holy Spirit, which is the doorway to being filled with the power of God. We should continue being filled so that we can operate in both the natural and supernatural gifting of the kingdom.

"Now to each one the manifestation of the Spirit is given for the common good. To one there is given through the Spirit a message of wisdom, to another a message of knowledge by means of the same Spirit, to another faith by the same Spirit, to another gifts of healing by that one Spirit, to another miraculous powers, to another prophecy, to another distinguishing between spirits, to another speaking in different kinds of tongues, and to still another the interpretation of tongues. All these are the work of one and the same Spirit, and he distributes them to each one, just as he determines." 1 Corinthians 12:7-11

"So, in Christ, we, though many, form one body, and each member belongs to all the others. We have different gifts, according to the grace given to each of us. If your gift is prophesying, then prophesy in accordance with your faith; if it is serving, then serve; if it is teaching, then teach; if it is to encourage, then give encouragement; if it is giving, then give generously; if it is to lead, do it diligently; if it is to show mercy, do it cheerfully." Romans 12:5-8

Some of these gifts are evident in today's church but where are the rest? God's children are supposed to have supernatural provision but there are obstacles in the way. The evil one wants to stop the flow of God's love, anointing and power flowing through the body and transforming lives. So, we must get the Royal Law in place and stop making a truce with sinful habits. What is a truce? It is inadvertently making a treaty with the devil by allowing him to still govern part of your behaviour.

It is time to claim victory in the areas where you have made a truce. Just keep moving in the right direction.

Dr. Martin Luther King Jr. used to tell his civil rights workers,

'If you can't fly, run. If you can't run, walk. If you can't walk, crawl, but by all means keep moving.'

Jim Elliot once observed that many Christians are so intent on doing something for God that they forget God's main work is to make something of them.

It is in fact to get us to live our lives out of the foundation of the Royal Law.

All that you have around you has no permanence so learn to think differently about it. Forever is forever and you will be alive forevermore. Allow this to govern your choices. It's as simple as this - each day set your goals to love God by loving people. Give yourself a reminder that this is truly what God is looking for and He will cause every good thing to come your way if only you will keep His commands to love. In this is our victory over the cosmos and its god (Satan)!

Remember, everything that our senses reveal to us is only temporary. The born again person is a citizen of another place. The more I live and see what this cosmos does to people, the more delighted I am that I am indeed a citizen of another place.

CHAPTER NINE
CITIZENS OF HEAVEN

"But our citizenship is in Heaven and we eagerly await a Saviour from there, the Lord Jesus Christ." Philippians 3:20

The word "citizenship" is very important here because it signifies something special. It signifies a colony of foreigners who, though living in a foreign country, live by the laws of their own country and model their lives after their native home.

Philippi was of course a Roman colony whose inhabitants, though not actually in Rome, lived as though they were. They dressed like Romans, talked like Romans and even thought like Romans. If we go to most parts of the world we will see the British doing the same. At the moment I am writing this in Arusha, Tanzania, our former home - we are now setting up home in Tanga, another Tanzanian City. One of the beauties of Tanzania is that it is still possible to observe a culture that has not been tarnished by the modern world. There are many people living today as their ancestors lived thousands of years ago. Still, even here, the ex-pat community shows signs of their European way of life. In other words we maintain the culture of another place in the face of the abiding culture and ways.

So Paul's statement *citizens of heaven* meant that we are to live according to the laws of heaven rather than the laws of earth.

Heaven and its blessings are **now** in terms of our spiritual experience. The oxygen of the kingdom is *agape*.

"By this will all men know that we are His disciples, that we have love (agape) one for another…" John 13:35

Is this how the world recognises us? If not then why not? Have we missed something?

"Praise be to the God and Father of our Lord Jesus Christ, who has blessed us in the heavenly realms, with every spiritual blessing in Christ." Ephesians 1:3

The location of these blessings is "The heavenlies". That is where Christ is seated.

"That power is the same as the mighty strength He exerted in Christ when He raised Him from the dead and seated Him at His right hand in the heavenly realms." Ephesians 1:20

This is also where the believer is seated.

"And God raised us up with Christ and seated us with Him in the heavenly realms in Christ Jesus." Ephesians 2:6

It is also the place of blessings.

"Who has blessed us in the heavenly realms with every spiritual blessing in Christ."

Every...

We are to learn how to bring each of heaven's blessings into the earth's atmosphere

"For our struggle is not against flesh and blood but against the rulers, against the authorities, against the powers of this dark world and against the spiritual forces of evil in the heavenly realms." Ephesians 6:12

Now if these were the blessings of God in the 'earthly realm' as opposed to the 'heavenly realm' then they could be obtained by earthly means. But as they are located in the 'heavenly realm' they can be acquired by heavenly means only. If we are to bring the blessings of God to earth, we must live by the laws of heaven. If you keep the laws of heaven you will keep the laws of the land, because the laws of heaven are centred on loving your fellow man by the highest form of love. This, even when he doesn't deserve it! God has deposited the riches of heaven in our account, but unless we know how to write cheques on that account we will spend our days in spiritual poverty.

So the big question is, how? How do we move the blessings of heaven into our earth now? How do we make what is ours positionally, ours experientially? How, having been rooted and established in *agape*, can we draw on the vast wealth that is now available to us direct from heaven?

The answer to all these 'how's' is the same. It's faith!

But…

"The only thing that counts is faith expressing itself through love (agape)." Galatians 5:6

Faith is the substance from heaven – love is the law of heaven. The two are intrinsically linked. Everything that Christ has done for the believer is absolute but it must be appropriated. Absolute means: 'perfectly independent of anything else to sustain it, self existent and unlimited'; appropriate means 'to take as one's own – to take possession'. All of God's promises are absolute, *"yes and amen."* So the sacrificial death of Christ is absolute in that nothing else is required for man's salvation and that His death is on behalf of every man. God's love, in Christ, was directed to the whole world.

"For God so loved the world that he gave his one and only son." John 3:16

"Look, the Lamb of God, who takes away the sin of the world." John 1:29

"He is the atoning sacrifice for our sins, and not only for ours, but also for the sins of the whole world." 1 John 2:2

This absolute atonement has to be appropriated by faith.

In simple terms, believing activates the promise...

"He who does not believe stands condemned already." John 3:18

If we can understand this principle then we can understand the principle of faith. We receive because we believe and because we act on what we believe. When Jesus came to earth He began to preach,

"The Kingdom of God is at hand."

His message was, the age to come has come and He demonstrated it by His power over disease, the devil and death. These two ages run side by side – the age to come began some 2000 years ago in Bethlehem. That's why Colossians 1:13 says we have already been delivered from the dominion of darkness:

"For He has rescued us from the dominion of darkness and into the kingdom of the Son He loves." Colossians 1:13

We have tasted some of the powers of the coming age but not yet all the powers of the coming age – maybe it is time we did.

Jesus Himself taught us to pray,

"Your will be done on earth as it is in heaven."

Obviously heaven can touch earth now or this prayer is a mockery. However, heaven's blessings will only come to earth now to the degree that we live by heaven's laws now. Bible teacher J. Oswald Sanders said, 'The function of faith is to turn God's promises into fact'. I say a fact is only a fact until it comes up against a higher reality. Live the Royal Law, pray for the promise, and believe that you will receive it, act on what God tells you to do and you will receive what you have asked for. It is meant to be that dynamic for all believers.

Here is the Scriptural evidence,

"Therefore, I tell you, whatever you ask for in prayer, believe that you have received it and it will be yours. And when you stand praying, if you hold anything against anyone, forgive him so that your heavenly father may forgive your sins." Mark 11:24-25

More about this later!

We can see that the Royal Law links heaven to earth and earth back to heaven. Living by heaven's law opens the door for the promise of God to be realised on earth. Confidence is built when we live as citizens of heaven now during our sojourn on earth. The greatest way to reflect that is love. It is *agape* that sets us apart and *agape* that empowers us. Once we are receiving the promises of God it ought to be obvious to all who are in contact with our lives. You and I are God's best evangelistic programme. Do people want what they see you have?

How much time and effort should we be putting into the cultivation of the Royal Law?

CHAPTER 10
LOVE LETTERS

"You yourselves are our letter, written on our hearts, known and read by everyone." 2 Corinthians 3:2

The living God is here for us always - *an ever present help in times of need.* Sometimes we will need to rely on His power and authority – sometimes we will need to rely on His wisdom to gain His perspective. Do people see the reality of your faith? Do they see that you are stable and walk in authority, power, wisdom and understanding? God intended that you should be a letter. When people read you they should at all times read what you are capable of. You are certainly capable of love, don't aim for things that you are not capable of in yourself, aim for things that you are and the rest will surely follow.

"You, yourselves are our letter, written on our hearts, known and read by everyone. You show that you are a letter from Christ, the result of our ministry, written not with ink but with the Spirit of the living God, not on tablets of stone but on tablets of human hearts."
2 Corinthians 3:2-3

We should be prepared to be read, by God, quietly, but at times, by people, out loud. This is discipleship! So often dark experiences are the way in which God will bring us to a place whereby we can accept His counsel coming to us through a human agent. Why do we allow so much pride to exist in our midst? It is surely a killer of life.

Because we have allowed people to choose whether to be a disciple or not we now have the scenario where those who want to be disciples carry a more tremendous weight than those who belong but who do not want to be disciples. I repeat: if you are a follower of Christ, you have an obligation to God and His body on earth. You are being read so what is being read? Perhaps we do not realise the significance of this. Once you become a Christian you will either gather or scatter people.

"We can be filled to all the fullness of Christ" so that *"we will be mature and complete, not lacking anything."* James1:4

95

Nobody but you can stop this happening. So is this what is being read in you? We should not be satisfied until this is what people read in us. Light up your neighbourhood by fulfilling your obligation to God. To love at His level is both the minimum and maximum requirement.

This is another reason why we face trials. God knows human nature only too well – we will not grow until we are stretched. We must continue to be stretched so that we can contain more of God. And this means we must place ourselves in a position where we will be stretched. The person who has been severely stretched will accept God on His terms – nothing else is important. I know because I have been there.

Two things are important here:

1) We must learn to walk a straight line despite the trials and circumstances that beset us.

2) The reason for this is that we are *living letters* read by all.

God wants us to be an alternative society, which is achieved by adopting the ways of the kingdom of God, thus, leading us to be a counter-culture and not simply a sub-culture.

Under the Old Covenant, God raised up one nation, Israel, and gave them His Law. They were the only nation on earth who had the Law of God. God told them that if they kept the Law they would be a chosen nation amongst nations and all other nations would see that they were a counter-culture, thereby recognising God through this one nation.

Only the keeping of the entire Law, as given through Moses, and recorded in Deuteronomy, would give them the nature that God required. They had to keep every single part of it. They would be like a living letter read by the nations. Of course, as intended by God, they failed to do this (He knew that it was impossible). Thus, entered the new covenant through the shedding of the blood of God's Son, Jesus Christ. Now the church was to be the counter-culture but instead of keeping the Mosaic Law, the new covenant people were simply to keep the Royal Law. The very nature of Christ would be imparted into the believer so that all believers could live out the Royal Law through a process of believing and making choices to walk in the spirit.

Aren't you glad that our God doesn't say, 'If you hate and try to wipe out the heathen, the world will know you belong to me?'

Rather He says,

"Do not judge, and you will not be judged. Do not condemn, and you will not be condemned. Forgive and you will be forgiven. Give, and it will be given to you. A good measure, pressed down, shaken together and running over, will be poured into your lap. For with the measure you use, it will be measured to you." Luke 6:37-38

"We know that we have passed from death to life because we love (agape) our brothers. Anyone who does not love (agape) remains in death."
1 John 3:14

We owe a debt of love at this level.

On the eve of my going into hospital, which subsequently led to my darkest days, I had a dream whereby Debbie and I were facing creatures that we had never seen before. We could not escape them and didn't know what to do about them. This seemed to go on for an age and gradually became worse until I was experiencing a nightmare. It seemed like nothing I could do could help me until suddenly the presence of God came on the scene and brought peace in the midst of the chaos. The following morning the words 'When the presence comes the problems will disappear' were implanted in my spirit. This is how we receive from God even if the receipt of such things brings no immediate relief or victory. The seed of victory has now been sown into the spirit.

Around that time I also had a vision in which I was sitting in a stately home with God. I was in a very big room that resembled a library. In the background was a wall-library that contained all the knowledge that mankind had gleaned since the creation. This wall of books seemed never ending and was hugely impressive.

That is, until I looked at God who was sitting between the books and me. As I looked from this angle the books became minuscule in the light of His presence. Secondly, on the table was a globe atlas of the world. It impressed me as the biggest globe atlas I had seen, then God picked it up and it became minuscule in the palm of His hand. The final thing I saw was a jigsaw laid flatly on the table. The jigsaw was of human DNA. God quickly finished the puzzle and it lay complete on the table but it was only as God breathed on it that it became three-dimensional and took upon itself a life.

God was speaking to me about seeing Him in a dimension that I had never seen Him in before. In order to come out of my darkness I would have to find Him in this dimension. The fact, however, remains, when revelation lands in the spirit of a person it may not initially bring about change. This is because it has landed in seed form and it is only as the seed is watered and begins to germinate that the results appear. This truth became implanted in my heart over a period of time. What a vital living lesson.

CHAPTER ELEVEN
DELIVERED OUT OF LAW

"For you are not under Law but under grace." Romans 6:14

The Law cannot and indeed was never meant to save us. I have already mentioned this but let's look at it more fully.

The following Scripture passage needs to be read carefully for clarity.

Hebrews 7:11; 13-28

"If perfection could have been attained through the Levitical priesthood—and indeed the law given to the people, established that priesthood—why was there still need for another priest to come, one in the order of Melchizedek, not in the order of Aaron? He of whom these things are said belonged to a different tribe, and no one from that tribe has ever served at the altar. For it is clear that our Lord descended from Judah, and in regard to that tribe Moses said nothing about priests. And what we have said is even clearer if another priest like Melchizedek appears, one who has become a priest not on the basis of a regulation as to his ancestry but on the basis of the power of an indestructible life. For it is declared: "You are a priest forever, in the order of Melchizedek." The former regulation is set aside because it was weak and useless (for the law made nothing perfect), and a better hope is introduced, by which we draw near to God. And it was not without an oath! Others became priests without any oath, but he became a priest with an oath when God said to him: "The Lord has sworn and will not change his mind: 'You are a priest forever.'" Because of this oath, Jesus has become the guarantor of a better covenant. Now, there have been many of those priests, since death prevented them from continuing in office; but because Jesus lives forever, he has a permanent priesthood. Therefore he is able to save completely those who come to God through him, because he always lives to intercede for them. Such a high priest truly meets our need, one who is holy, blameless, pure, set apart from sinners, exalted above the heavens. Unlike the

other high priests, he does not need to offer sacrifices day after day, first for his own sins, and then for the sins of the people. He sacrificed for their sins once for all when he offered himself. For the law appoints as high priests men in all their weakness; but the oath, which came after the law, appointed the Son, who has been made perfect forever."

I repeat, the Law of God cannot save and was never meant to do so. It is, in fact, impossible to please God by trying to keep His law. I want to explain this by looking at the three priesthoods referred to in Scripture.

"If perfection could have been attained through the Levitical priesthood—and indeed the law given to the people, established that priesthood—why was there still need for another priest to come, one in the order of Melchizedek, not in the order of Aaron?"

The first is the mysterious figure Melchizedek whose name means king of righteousness, high priest over the gentiles.

We first meet Melchizedek in Genesis 14:18,

"Then Melchizedek king of Salem brought out bread and wine. He was Priest of God most high."

Then again in Psalm 110:4

This Priesthood was from the beginning - before there were any Jews on earth. Therefore, it was a priesthood for the non-Jew." (A gentile means non-Jew, those who had no covenant with God).

The second priesthood was the Levitical Priesthood, which was in the line of Aaron (Moses brother). This was the priesthood over the Jews, it was formed as the Jews became a nation and was for Jews alone.

The third priesthood was Jesus Christ Himself, who is the great high priest over Jew and Gentile and came in the order of Melchizedek.

"Therefore, there is now no condemnation for those who are in Christ Jesus, because through Christ Jesus the law of the Spirit who gives life has set you free from the law of sin and death. For what the law was powerless to do because it was, weakened by the flesh, God did by sending his own Son in the likeness of sinful flesh to be a sin offering. And so he condemned sin in the flesh." Romans 8:1-3

The Law is a religious thing but it is not a Christian thing. Through man's lack of understanding we have embraced the Law into Christendom when there is something far superior for us.

Zechariah, the father of John the Baptist was the last in the line of the Levitical priests. The priesthood had become generally corrupted as the Romans, the occupying force, had appointed the present high priest. Therefore, the uncorrupted John the Baptist was the one who baptised Jesus.

If growth came by the keeping of the Law the method God would use to enable us to grow would simply be the keeping of the Law - a set of rules! However, because this was never his intention, He has a far better method to enable us to grow.

Often, we really grow when God appears to have distanced Himself from us. When we have to search for Him and take measures that we have never had to take before. For example: when Jesus stood on the water and said to Peter, 'get out of the boat and come,' just as long as Peter had his mind set on what he was heading to he managed to walk on water but as soon as his mind wandered to the fact that he was defying nature - he began to sink.

Faith always enables us to do more than we could otherwise do.

I know through my only military service that we are capable, even in the natural man, of going much further than we think we can. The elite Special Air Services (SAS) of the British Army do much of their training on the Brecon Beacons in South Wales. One part of their training is to do long, excruciating marches through rough terrain and carrying heavy kit. The SAS pride themselves on both their physical and mental fitness and they are among the most elite troops in the world. It is known that as the soldiers think they have finished their marches and arrive at their recovery trucks in a state of exhaustion they think they have finished. But that's not the end, the trucks drive off forcing the soldiers to go further than they imagined they would and, more important, than they thought they could.

Aged 52 I reached the summit of Mount Kilimanjaro, the world's highest freestanding mountain. It was ten years after I had been forced to leave Tanzania with my heart condition that I accomplished this. It took six days and in truth I was almost defeated on the first day. One of the greatest lessons I learned on the climb was to 'see it through'.

Real growth comes when we allow God to stretch our faith - so he sets up the process by using trials, challenges and circumstances - all off a basis of unconditional love.

You can yet go much further than you thought you would or could and you should. Ask: what is my bulls-eye? What do I yet want to achieve in my life that will be pleasing to God?

Catch the following and you will go and do much more than you thought was possible:

"Your faith, which is of greater worth than gold." 1 Peter 1:7

Have you understood that? *'Greater worth than gold.'*

Romans 10:4 informs us,

"Christ is the end of the law so that there may be righteousness for everyone who believes."

Note: *who believes.*

Jesus Christ came in the order of Melchizedek not Aaron.

"But now a righteousness, from God, apart from Law, has been made known, to which the Law and the prophets testify. This righteousness from God comes through faith in Jesus Christ to all who believe there is no difference." Romans 3:21

So what then was God's purpose in giving the Levitical Law through Moses?

This is answered for us in Romans 3:19, which says,

"Now we know that whatever the Law says, it says to those who are under the Law so that every mouth may be silenced and the whole world held accountable to God. Therefore, no one will be declared righteous in His sight by observing the Law; rather through the Law we become conscious of sin."

There can be no conversion without conviction - this is how God makes use of the Law.

"For all have sinned and fall short of the glory of God." Romans 3:23

There is the damning conviction.

Here comes the amazing grace,

"And are justified freely by His grace through the redemption that came by Christ Jesus." Romans 3:24

This Christ is now able to save completely those who come to Him - whether they are Jew, Hindu, Muslim or nothing.

Listen again: Hebrews 7:23-28

"Now there have been many of those priests, since death prevented them from continuing in office; but because Jesus lives forever, he has a permanent priesthood. Therefore, He is able to save completely those who come to God through Him, because He always lives to intercede for them. Such a High Priest meets our need - one who is holy, blameless, pure, set apart from sinners, exalted above the heavens. Unlike the other high priests, he does not need to offer sacrifices day after day, first for his own sins, and then for the sins of the people. He sacrificed for their sins once for all when He offered Himself. For the Law appoints as high priest men who are

weak; but the oath, which came after the Law, appointed the Son, who has been made perfect forever."

Folks, you are not under law, you are under grace and you also have a great high priest who is interceding for you. You are heaven bound forever. If He has done all this on earth for you imagine what it will be like in heaven.

You are heading for heaven but eternal life begins now. Because of grace you can enjoy it to the fullest degree. We are going to see the extravagant expectations of those who are seeking to keep the Royal Law, which is the doorway into Promised Land living.

Surely, our obedience on earth will gain His intercession for us in heaven. It does, therefore, it will. What a thought that is! No wonder we should attempt things for Him, through obeying the Great Commission. Be excited, His intercession will have a profound effect on your future.

"Commit your plans to the Lord and they will succeed." Proverbs 16:3

"No good thing will He will withhold from Him whose walk is blameless." Psalm 84:11

Those two verses thrill me because I know how to fulfill the requirement: it is *agape.*

CHAPTER TWELVE
GOING FURTHER THAN WE'VE EVER BEEN

"I can do all things through Christ who strengthens me."
Philippians 4:13

God will put immense pressure on us so that we will go further than we've ever been. Maybe that is why he has led you to this book. If you think so, contact us and we'll try to help you further.

I was once on a panel in a church in Brighton and was posed the following question:

'How have you known that you were equipped to do the things you've done? That is: entering pastoral ministry relatively quickly after conversion (considering the past I'd had) and taking your young family to the third world mission field.'

My answer was unrehearsed and surprised me in the speed in which I articulated it:

' I sent my heart ahead of me and then learned to do it en-route.'

That was the truth. I don't believe we can ever do what God asks us to do. Without Him that is!

"Man does not live on bread alone but by every word that proceeds from the mouth of God." Luke 4:4

Notice something here, *does not.* However well we may be living we are not living to our maximum potential unless we are living by every word that proceeds from the mouth of God. I know that I have not yet become all that I am.

The Bible tells us,

"The word of God is living and active." Hebrews 4:12

And in John 6:63

"The Spirit gives life the flesh counts for nothing the words I have spoken are Spirit and they are life."

If bread (food) provides us with life and health - then can God's word have the same affect? I think so! The word is the equipper.

"My son pay attention to my words, do not let them out of your sight, for they are life to those who find them and health to a man's whole body." Proverbs 4:20

That is quite a claim isn't it? The word of God equates to life and health; so don't let it out of your sight. It is my wholehearted belief that, if we are keeping the Royal Law, then we can expect to receive life, health and all things from the word of God. The connection is *agape* love, which is God's frequency.

Scientific healing comes from outside of us in the form of medication and the skills of the medical profession. But has God devised a way by which we can receive healing through His word and His Spirit on the inside?

"Seek first the Kingdom of God and His righteousness and all these things will be added unto you." Matthew 6:63

How do we do this? Well we do it by getting hold of the keys of the Kingdom. Take the keys and unlock the doorway into the riches and resources of the kingdom. Note this says, keys of the Kingdom not keys to the Kingdom. Having gained entrance to the Kingdom through Jesus Christ there has to be a taking, a pressing in, a getting hold of the keys of the Kingdom. We need to know what gives us access to the riches of the Kingdom. Having gained access to the kingdom, truly living in it is what counts.

Dallas Willard says, 'we need a key of the keys.' So what is that key of the keys?

The Apostle Paul wrote,

"I pray that the eyes of your heart would be enlightened (opened) that you may know..." Ephesians 1:18

The natural eye sees circumstances and forms its pictures of reality. The eyes of your heart see reality and allow it to determine vision, aspect and status. The abundance of God is not passively received and does not happen by chance. The abundance of God is claimed and put into action by our active, intelligent pursuit of it.

May we gain and maintain access. The Lord won't manifest His presence just because you sing, pray, read or even give. He will manifest His presence because of who you are, followed by what you do. The real cosmic battle is not out there; it is inside of us. We should wage war against pride, against rebellion, against indifference, against unbelief, against a casual indifference to our own sin and against our unwillingness to keep the Royal Law. The Royal Law is not a set of rules to be kept, it is an attitude of heart and a willingness to take responsibility to think and act a certain way. We are commanded to do this but it's outworking has one golden rule: *"do unto others, as you would have them do for you."*

Aren't you glad that God wants people to treat you like that? God's commands are given to protect human life not to put limits on it and spoil it. He commands us all to treat one another with love and respect. We are so precious to Him that He demands nothing less and makes clear that there are dire consequences in not doing so.

Love your neighbour as you love yourself is not a polite request or indication of a good idea - it is a command. What are we denying ourselves by failing to keep the Royal Law? Once the eyes of our hearts are opened, we gain access to understanding, both the universe within as well as the universe without. Outside of God we will not have balance - our pursuit of understanding one will cause us to neglect and misunderstand the other.

"That you might know the hope to which he has called you, his glorious inheritance in the saints and His incomparable power for us who believe." Ephesians 1:19

What is your point of view? Think on those words, 'point of view'. What you see is determined by what you are looking out from. Our aim should be that we press into God until we can see through the eyes of our hearts.

"For my thoughts are not your thoughts, neither are your ways my ways," declares the Lord. "As the heavens are higher than the earth, so are my ways higher than your ways and my thoughts than your thoughts. As the rain and the snow come down from heaven, and do not return to it without watering the earth and making it bud and flourish, so that it yields seed for the sower and bread for the eater, so is my word that goes out from my mouth: It will not return to me empty, but will accomplish what I desire and achieve the purpose for which I sent it." Isaiah 55:8-11

As high as the heavens are above the earth that's a long way. So is it possible to understand God except through the eyes of the heart? The eyes of the heart interpret for the spirit; the natural eyes interpret for the soul. The soul is restored and God conquers our inner space when we draw close enough to interpret through the eyes (understanding) of the heart. God is often further than the physical eyes can see, making it an impossibility to understand what he is doing apart from faith.

The one key that gives access to all other keys is of course the Royal Law - love at God's intended level. Can we give him enough of our inner space so that we can love at His level? How, in practice do we do this?

Here is the best, in my opinion; most incise, passage of Scripture to explain it,

"I am the true vine, and my Father is the gardener. He cuts off every branch in me that bears no fruit, while every branch that does bear fruit he prunes so that it will be even more fruitful. You are already clean because of the word I have spoken to you. Remain in me, as I also remain in you. No branch can bear fruit by itself; it must remain in the vine. Neither can you bear fruit unless you remain in me. I am the vine; you are the branches. If you remain in me and I in you, you will bear much fruit; apart from me you can do nothing.

If you do not remain in me, you are like a branch that is thrown away and withers; such branches are picked up, thrown into the fire and burned. If you remain in me and my words remain in you, ask whatever you wish, and it will be done for you. This is to my Father's glory, that you bear much fruit, showing yourselves to be my disciples. As the Father has loved me, so I have loved you. Now remain in my love. If you keep my commands, you will remain in my love, just as I have kept my Father's commands and remain in his love. I have told you this so that my joy may be in you and that your joy may be complete. My command is this: Love each other as I have loved you. Greater love has no one than this: to lay down one's life for one's friends. I no longer call you servants, because a servant does not know his master's business. Instead, I have called you friends, for everything that I learned from my Father I have made known to you. You did not choose me, but I chose you and appointed you so that you might go and bear fruit—fruit that will last—and so that whatever you ask in my name the Father will give you. This is my command: Love each other."
John 15:1-17

How do we remain in Him? By remaining in His love,

"If you keep my commands, you will remain in my love, just as I have kept my Father's commands and remain in his love."

There is another way of dealing with what you are dealing with right now. Why be limited by the boundaries of the third dimension when you have access to a greater dimension? Our time and energy should be given over to the cultivation of love at His required level. That is our understanding and application of *agape*.

"I have told you this so that my joy may be in you and that your joy may be complete. My command is this: Love each other as I have loved you. Greater love has no one than this: to lay down one's life for one's friends."

Agape love increases power because love is the power. They are inseperable. He died for you so that you would love for Him. Will you pause for a moment just to realise how much God loves people. This life is meant to introduce us to the real thing, which lasts forever. Aren't you glad you have made it to the real thing? This means you are living forever.

"I no longer call you servants, because a servant does not know his master's business. Instead, I have called you friends, for everything that I learned from my Father I have made known to you. You did not choose me, but I chose you and appointed you so that you might go and bear fruit—fruit that will last—and so that whatever you ask in my name the Father will give you. This is my command: Love each other."

If you do this one thing, you can ask and receive anything. If you don't do this one thing, then what you get will be limited in respect to what Jesus died to give you.

Listen: *"man cannot live on bread alone."*

CHAPTER THIRTEEN
ON AND IN THROUGH OBEDIENCE

"If you obey my commands you are really my disciples, then, you shall know the truth and the truth will set you free." John 15:10

It is time now to take a leap forward. Now that you have had either a reminder or first time revelation of the importance of the commands to love at God's required level, it is time to press on and establish yourself in the Promised Land.

We have learned that the foundation of the Royal Law - appropriating faith, which leads to obedience - is the key that releases heaven's blessing into the earth's atmosphere. The Israelites had wandered in the wilderness for 40 years on their way from Egypt to Canaan - the Promised Land. The journey could have taken a mere two weeks. The reason for this delay is explained in the following,

"The Israelites had moved about in the desert forty years until all the men who were of military age when they left Egypt had died, since they had not obeyed The Lord. For The Lord had sworn to them that they would not see the land that He had solemnly promised their fathers to give us, a land flowing with milk and honey." Joshua 5:6

And in Deuteronomy 8:2,

"Remember how the Lord your God led you all the way in the wilderness these forty years, to humble and test you in order to know what was in your heart, whether or not you would keep his commands. He humbled you, causing you to hunger and then feeding you with manna, which neither you nor your ancestors had known, to teach you that man does not live on bread alone but on every word that comes from the mouth of the Lord."

In reading the history of these forty years of wilderness wandering two things emerge,

The Israelites did not obey God's word. The Israelites failed to go in and invade the land.

This principle is always the same.

We might say fear and unbelief led to disobedience! The three obstacles to advancing are always sin, fear or doubt. The Israelites underestimated God's ability. Out of all the Israelites set free from Egypt only two men actually went on to live in the Promised Land, namely, Joshua and Caleb. All of them were set free under the same terms but only two found out that the promises of God were true - thousands upon thousands missed out on Promised Land living. They missed out because they were judging things through natural reasoning rather than by faith. Joshua and Caleb were among twelve spies (representatives) sent in to spy out the Promised Land. Only these two men said that the Land could be taken, even though God had promised the land to them. Fear that the promises of God are not true is the snare that leads to disobedience, which in turn leads to missing out on living in the Promised Land. God acts when we obey His word - obedience unlocks and activates the promises. The tragedy is that the thousands upon thousands who did not enter could have done so if only they would have trusted God's word.

'Faith is not a product of the reasoning faculties, but of the recreated spirit.' (author unknown).

We are about to understand what they would have seen (manifest) if only they had obeyed God's word. Remember, they greatly feared the Canaanites who lived in the Promised Land. This fear of obeying God, due to reasoning, rather than standing on the promises of God's word, would cost them beyond measure. They had not understood how God would do it so they reasoned He wouldn't or couldn't. This despite what the word promised. Are we the same? Their first task in taking the Promised Land was a major one. It was to cross the River Jordan but they had not reckoned on the following,

"For the Lord your God dried up the Jordan before you until you had crossed over. The Lord your God did to the Jordan what he had done to the Red Sea when he dried it up before us until we had crossed over. He did this so that all the peoples of the earth might

know that the hand of the Lord is powerful and so that you might always fear the Lord your God." Joshua. 4:23-24

You would have thought that the Israelites would have trusted God due to what He had done in the past. He had dried up the Red Sea - could he not now then dry up the River Jordan? They had seen how supernaturally He works to fulfil His word and carry out His promises when His word is obeyed,

"Moses lift up your staff..."

This was the strange instruction that Moses received from God as the Israelites were trapped on the shores of the Red Sea. The result was: the sea parted and they passed through safely.

When God repeated this miracle by drying up the River Jordan, look what happened to the thing the Israelites feared, namely, the Amorites and Canaanites.

"Now when all the Amorite kings west of the Jordan and all the Canaanite kings along the coast heard how the Lord had dried up the Jordan before the Israelites until they had crossed over, their hearts melted in fear and they no longer had the courage to face the Israelites." Joshua 5:1

Wow! God took care of that one. We can say with surety, the battle belongs to The Lord. Remember, figuratively speaking, God doesn't usually use bridges (they crossed a sea and a river without bridges) often his promises are fulfilled through supernatural means. This is how God dealt with the things they feared. It was God who took care of the enemy and not the Israelites. He simply sought their obedience as He does ours. Surely, He is looking for a people who will have enough faith to love at His intended level. After all, he commanded it!

God knew that they had no need to fear because he knows the future. He simply asks us to trust and obey his word to us. He will keep His word but until you understand and are rooted and established in love, Satan will always be able to get in and cause you to doubt or misinterpret the goodness of God's word, as it pertains to you. If you are walking in the awareness of incredibly good news it will become obvious to the onlookers that you are. When we obey His word he removes the obstacles.

Having entered the land and knowing that their enemies no longer had the courage to face them one would have thought that they would have rampaged through, taking the land but God had different ideas in Joshua 5:2 he told Joshua,

"Make flint knives and circumcise the Israelites again. So, Joshua made flint knives and circumcised the Israelites at Gibeath Haaraloth."

And in verse 4,

"Now this is why he did so: all those who came out of Egypt - all the men of military age - died in the desert on the way after leaving Egypt."

The rite of circumcision marked Israel's position as God's covenant people. When God made the original covenant with Abraham, He required that each male would be circumcised as a sign of cutting off the old life and beginning the new. The ones who didn't enter the Promised Land were in covenant with God; the promises were theirs, yet they failed to unlock the promises through their disobedience. It was indeed a tragedy but God's plan wasn't thwarted, He simply raised up the next generation. He will always do what He has promised to do, yet, tragically so many of His people miss out on what He has promised to do because of lack of obedience.

God gives the sign of the Covenant to the next generation. They are circumcised and then they celebrate the Passover for the first time in a long time and only the third time in 40 years.

"On the evening of the fourteenth day of the month, while camped at Gilgal on the plains if Jericho the Israelites celebrated the Passover." Joshua 5:10

Isn't it a strange way to conduct war, the Israelites invade Canaan, set up camp two miles from Jericho and were then told by God to stop, circumcise the men then celebrate the Passover?

The principle is this, when we obey God He brings about the victory. Stand firm and see your deliverance. Trust, follow and obey. Look at this considering the diet they had been on for forty years.

"The day after the Passover, that very day, they ate some of the produce of the land: unleavened bread and roasted grain."
Joshua 5:11

What's the significance of this? Well, God had promised a land to them that was bountiful. Remember, they had been in the desert for 40 years and God had miraculously supplied Manna for them to eat. In the bountiful Promised Land they no longer needed this miraculous supply because the Promised Land was ready for harvesting and planting. It was just as He had promised. We can enter our own promised land by obeying God. After all, we have His promises. I'm willing you to do so; I'm urging you on. Not just for your sake but for the sake of the Kingdom of God.

Those who did not enter due to fear and disobedience could not foresee the following. God had promised therefore God was in control of the situation. Circumcise the men then celebrate the Passover. They had feared the natural circumstances to the degree that they couldn't trust the word of God on the matter. So, they failed to enter. However, for those who did enter, this is what they experienced,

"Now when all the Amorite kings west of the Jordan and all the Canaanite kings along the coast heard how the Lord had dried up the Jordan before the Israelites until they had crossed over, their hearts melted in fear and they no longer had the courage to face the Israelites. Now when Joshua was near Jericho, he looked up and saw a man standing in front of him with a drawn sword in his hand. Joshua went up to him and asked, "Are you for us or for our enemies?" "Neither," he replied, "but as commander of the army of the Lord I have now come." Then Joshua fell facedown to the ground in reverence, and asked him, "What message does my Lord

have for his servant?" The commander of the Lord's army replied, "Take off your sandals, for the place where you are standing is holy And Joshua did so. Now the gates of Jericho were securely barred because of the Israelites. No one went out and no one came in. Then the Lord said to Joshua, See, I have delivered Jericho into your hands, along with its king and its fighting men. March around the city once with all the armed men. Do this for six days. Have seven priests carry trumpets of rams' horns in front of the ark.

On the seventh day, march around the city seven times, with the priests blowing the trumpets. When you hear them sound a long blast on the trumpets, have the whole army give a loud shout; then the wall of the city will collapse and the army will go up, everyone straight in. So Joshua son of Nun called the priests and said to them, "Take up the ark of the covenant of the Lord and have seven priests carry trumpets in front of it." And he ordered the army, "Advance! March around the city, with an armed guard going ahead of the ark of the Lord."
Joshua 5:13-6:6

We know the rest, the walls came down and the Israelites gained a total victory without loss. There is victory with loss and victory without loss due to obedience. I know which one is my preference.

You can enter your promised land because obedience is something you can carry out. Most of us struggle to obey God implicitly, because we don't really trust the outcome to God. My advice to you is, remove the doubt by fulfilling the Royal Law. This alone will give you unending confidence to trust God. It is my belief that we are living in the synergy of the ages. In a recent prayer meeting I felt I heard God say the following: 'you're standing on the edge of a million answered prayers.' Is this something that you can believe? If so, don't miss out; begin to put into practice the principles revealed in this book. Just remember, your status in Christ will always rescue your standing, so, I repeat, you have not yet become all that you are.

Look again at the significance of these words:

"Then the Lord said to Joshua, "See, I have delivered Jericho into your hands."

Joshua was faithful, he trusted God and obeyed His word. His example has touched millions of lives. The price of ill discipline is far greater than the price paid for discipline. The momentary pain of discipline and obedience can have eternal gain. We are to obey God and reason that He will work supernaturally to achieve for us what He has promised. If need be, God will, at the right time, create a miracle to accompany our obedience. God is outside of natural law and is not therefore restricted by it.

He can literally do anything any way He desires. The lesson to learn is: do not fear because you cannot see how God is going to do it. I repeat, God is not restricted by natural law, He can and will do what He has promised either conventionally or unconventionally.

CHAPTER FOURTEEN
CHOICES THAT LEAD TO POWER

"See I set before you today, life and prosperity,
death and destruction."
Deuteronomy 30:15

Maybe the time has come for you to make some choices. Are you ready? There is immense power in decision.

'The power of the process is determined by the depth of the decision.' (author unknown)

When King David went to fight Goliath, the narrative says that he left his baggage behind (he went with just a sling-shot) and went to slay Goliath. We can see some wonderful spiritual truth when we compare this episode with what happened in the life of David's predecessor, king Saul. In relation to my own life, I carried unnecessary baggage into the ministry and out on to the mission field. What a waste of energy it is to carry such weight. In the following Scripture verses we find that Saul is hiding among the baggage.

"So they inquired further of the Lord, "Has the man come here yet? And the Lord said, "Yes, he has hidden himself among the supplies."
1 Samuel 10:22

The point here is, if we hide amidst the baggage we will eventually return to what is in the baggage.

This could be:

Our own means
Sinful habits
Independence
Prideful thinking
Physical attributes
Personality

We are to be cleansed of our sin then purged of our self. We see in the narrative that Saul began again to rely on his own means. In the absence of the prophet Samuel, he makes a sacrifice to God. He knew full well that only the prophet should do this. The result was that God decided to replace Saul with David whom he described as a man after his own heart. It is more comfortable to hide among the baggage than it is to leave it behind and trust only in God for tomorrow. The reason is we have always trusted what is contained in the baggage.

Saul was hiding among the baggage and we see that God eventually showed the people where Saul was hiding. The truth is, we can generally see what is wrong with one another and that is why we discuss one another's faults. But because we have not learned to speak the truth in love it doesn't come into the open. This is why we need to have accountability and this is formed through discipleship formed through relationships.

What baggage would you have others who affect your life to put down?

What irritates you?

What about your spouse? If you could change them in any area and, it was in their power to change, what would you ask them to change? What about parents, friends, your pastor, leaders? What about your church?

Well, God is our best friend and understanding human nature as He does, He goes to great lengths, in His word, to tell us what we need to change.

How the baggage limits us!

Get someone to carry a heavy bag, then to carry an empty bag. The difference will determine a lot, like how far the person can go and in what manner they go. We hide among the baggage because we assume that everything we need is in the bag so we walk around with all kinds of excess weight weighing us down. It's kind of a 'just in case.' God wants you to know what and where you are going to and He wants you to do it without your baggage.

The Late Ed Cole once commented that winners focus on what they are going to, whilst losers focus on what they are going through. Peter walked on the water just as long as he focused on what he was going to. As soon as he didn't, he sank! Get in the centre of God's will, for being in God's will is infinitely better than anything the world has to offer.

"After this I looked, and there before me was a door standing open in heaven. And the voice I had first heard speaking to me, like a trumpet said, "Come up here, and I will show you what must take place after this." Revelation 4:1

Instead of relying on what's in your baggage start to knock on God's door.

"For everyone who asks receives; the one who seeks finds; and to the one who knocks, the door will be opened." Matthew 7:8

You will never be able to hear God clearly, in a particular area, until He has renewed your mind. It is time to do all that we can do to be transformed in our thinking. Every physical reality began its life as a thought. The building you are in, the car you drive, the book you hold began its life as an idea.

Victor Hugo famously said,

'An invasion of armies can be resisted, but not an idea whose time has come.'

We should lay down our baggage and in particular the baggage of wrong thinking that we have been both convinced of and believed to be right thinking.

Matthew 7:12 takes us to the crux of the matter, without doubt this needs to be understood.

"So in everything, do to others what you would have them do to you, for this sums up the Law and the Prophets."

We should treat others, as we would want to be treated had we done what they have done.

I have not always done this and I have also been on the receiving end of a lack of mercy, grace and understanding. It is, in my opinion, an Achilles heel of the church. We measure God's love by how people love us, we are undone because people don't love us as they should, so, we think God doesn't love us as He should.

"By this the world will know that you belong to me - the love (agape) you have for one another."

The church community is like no other; it should stand out in a world that cannot compete with its love, mercy, grace and forgiveness of one another. We want fairness but grace is not fair - it goes way beyond what is fair.

Giving
Recurring
Acceptance
Continually to
Everyone

One thing it has taken me a long time to grasp is God's grace toward me. I have carried lots of baggage in my thinking that could easily convince me that I haven't received on going grace when I need it most.

"For everyone who asks receives; the one who seeks finds; and to the one who knocks, the door will be opened." Matthew 7:8

As long as we act on the word of God we will receive.

'Do' (as in do unto others) is an active word it means start to do something for others. Because of our worth, God wants us to be treated like His children and that is best achieved when we, His children, grasp this and implement it on behalf of others. Do something unexpected for a person who you think doesn't deserve it - something you would dearly love them to do for you, particularly when you needed it most. The price that was paid for you and me is evidence of how much we are worth to God. This fact ought to tell us something. We must narrow the world of John 3:16 down to the individual.

"For God so loved John Bullock that He gave His only begotten son, so that if John believes in Him he shall not perish but have eternal life."

That is the price God was willing to pay because of your (my) worth.

"Can any one of you by worrying add a single hour to your life? And why do you worry about clothes? See how the flowers of the field grow. They do not labour or spin. Yet I tell you that not even Solomon in all his splendour was dressed like one of these. If that is how God clothes the grass of the field, which is here today and tomorrow is thrown into the fire, will he not much more clothe you— you of little faith?"
Matthew 6:27-30

The key to waiting through any situation is to trust, follow and obey. This process is the absolute opposite and antithesis of being governed by feelings and natural circumstances! Like never before you are ready to allow God to go much deeper within you. Here's how: allow God to take the inner space. So much research has gone into trying to understand the Universe or outer space but how much has gone into trying to understand inner space what makes us human beings tick from the inside? It is my belief that the way we see the environment on the outside can be completely transformed if we change the environment on the inside. Don't allow the paradigm (idea or concept) that you live under diminish your understanding of reality. Let's revisit a point I made earlier, all the knowledge, understanding and experience gathered in life can only be absorbed into the right foundation of what we are in essence. Right foundations, therefore, are imperative. The Scripture tells us that we are to be rooted and established in love (*agape*), nothing less...

Here is another quote (author unknown) that changed my paradigm, 'faith begins at the known will of God.' What do you believe is included in the atonement?

Coming to Christ gives us an opportunity to re-establish our foundations. However, it is likely that you have never properly done this.

"Now what I am commanding you today is not too difficult for you or beyond your reach. It is not up in heaven, so that you have to ask, "Who will ascend into heaven to get it and proclaim it to us so we may obey it?" Nor is it beyond the sea, so that you have to ask, "Who will cross the sea to get it and proclaim it to us so we may obey it?" No, the word is very near you; it is in your mouth and in your heart so you may obey it. See, I set before you today life and prosperity, death and destruction. For I command you today to love the Lord your God, to walk in obedience to him, and to keep his commands, decrees and laws; then you will live and increase, and the Lord your God will bless you in the land you are entering to possess." Deuteronomy 30:11-16

The enemy is waging psychological warfare against the body of Christ, constantly undermining us and holding us in the prison of our memories and in the limitations of strongholds. We are to be changed from glory to glory and this means allowing God into every area of our lives.

All forms of created life are based on cells. Cells are the building blocks of every living thing. The human body, contains about 100,000,000,000,000 cells (can you comprehend that number?) of which there are vast varieties. In his wisdom, God designated these cells to perform specific tasks. They work to order. Though they are invisible to the naked eye, cells are not (by far) the smallest particle known to man. Cells consist of numerous tinier structures called molecules, which are comprised of even smaller structures called elements and within elements can be found even tinier structures called atoms. Atoms are so small that this (.) full stop contains more than a billion of them. Yet, an atom is made up almost entirely of empty space. The remainder of the atom is made up of protons, neutrons and electrons. Protons and neutrons are clustered together in a minuscule nucleus at the very centre of the atom. Little bundles of energy called electrons storm around this nucleus at the speed of light. These core building blocks hold all things together.

Having understood those basic elements we need to further understand that they work to order. Scientists call this atomic energy. This term describes what they can't explain - a key to our understanding of life and its origins in the broader sense is, where does the atom get its energy? And, what is the force that holds it together? We must go to God's word for our answers. Hebrews 1:3 informs us,

"He is sustaining all things by the power of His Word."

Here we have it: the most powerful word in the Universe and it can be delivered through the mouth of the believer.

And, in Colossians 1:17

"In Him all things hold together."

God is the glue, the life force that holds all things together. So often we look at this Scripture in terms of our world out there (the universe without) and omit it from our understanding of our inner space (the universe within).

This amazing journey inside us is only part of the picture - this explains the physics of what makes man and it is extraordinary; but what about the inner space of our character, personality and temperament? This is the mind, the will and the emotions - the three components that make up the soul of man. The soul is the part of us that relates to our natural world but the spirit is the thing that ultimately transforms our characters by governing our souls. Until you come to Christ, your soul is rampant in its control of you.

The natural mind, will and emotions (that is before we come to Christ) are governed entirely by the environs dictating the on going formation of your character, personality and temperament. It is obvious from our understanding of Scripture that the well being of the natural elements can be greatly affected by the state of the spiritual. How far have we allowed the Spirit to transform us?

"Do not conform any longer to the pattern of this world but be transformed by the renewing of your mind." Romans 12:2

A great key in determining whether you will reach your potential in God or not - and that is no light thing - can be found in two words: conformed or transformed. Are you conformed to the pattern of this world or are you transformed by the renewing of your mind? My observations and personal experience lead me to believe that not many believers have been transformed to the degree that is desired by God. Whoever you are, whatever your background, whatever you have done. You must be transformed out of your natural culture and traditions into the culture of the kingdom of God. *Agape* will transform you and your capabilities.

The door into this is grace. The provision is the Word of God and the Holy Spirit and the means is the renewing of the mind. The real cosmic battle is not in the outer space but rather in the inner space. In terms of our outer space, the Bible clearly tells us what is out there. It is not a mystery!

"Finally, be strong in the Lord and in his mighty power. For our struggle is not against flesh and blood, but against the rulers, against the authorities, against the powers of this dark world and against the spiritual forces of evil in the heavenly realms." Ephesians 6:10, 12

So how do we fight this cosmic war? Well, not with nuclear bombs or guided missiles that's for sure. God has devised another way. You take this ground in accordance with the ground you have allowed God to take in you. The armour of God is His Word. It is the wearing of the Word. The more of His word we apply to our lives, the more ground we can potentially take. It is an inner work that leads to outward power.

"The weapons we fight with are not the weapons of the world. On the contrary, they have divine power to demolish strongholds. We demolish arguments and every pretension that sets itself up against

126

the knowledge of God, and we take captive every thought to make it obedient to Christ. And we will be ready to punish every act of disobedience, once your obedience is complete." 2 Corinthians 10:4-6

Real victory is linked to obedience to God's Word. Look at the link to this passage that we looked into in Romans 12:2

"Do not conform to the pattern of this world, but be transformed by the renewing of your mind. Then you will be able to test and approve what God's will is—his good, pleasing and perfect will."

If we can allow God to conquer the inner space of our lives we shall soon see how easy it is to conquer the outer space. His will is that we do so.

"And my God will do immeasurably more than all we can ask or imagine through His power that is at work within us." Ephesians 3:20

We can only conquer what is in the outer if we allow God to conquer what is in the inner. Renewal comes through a transformed mind. The most important things that should be understood about man and his world can't be taught in universities because these things are not understood merely through knowledge. They come through wisdom that is imparted through revelation. This revelation comes from none other than the creator and sustainer of the universe.

Charisma that has its source in the Spirit and flows through character is God's intention. However, there is another kind of charisma, it has its source in the soul and flows through personality. The latter has to maintain and build by using manipulation through personality. Rather than operate in the real anointing that affects the spirit, it operates out of hype, which affects the soul. To the immature both types of charisma appear to be the same. My hearts cry is not one of criticism but one of desire for the real thing. If we will cultivate our hearts and make it the goal of our lives to fulfil the Royal Law then we will allow God to take our inner space. As He takes our inner space, we will, in Him, begin to take the outer space, which consists of what is going on in the cosmos.

We are more than conquerors.

Let's live as such.

"Trust in The Lord with all your heart and lean not on your own understanding, acknowledge Him in all your ways and He will make your paths straight." Proverbs 3:5-6

Belief is in the integrity of God's Word. If God speaks then we can stand on what He says by faith. However, you cannot speak to a mountain and then interpret the result through sense knowledge. Truth is based on the fact that God does not lie; therefore, His Word is true. And if His word is true, then therein lays all the evidence that we need in order to interpret reality.

God's word has to be taken seriously. If God says, I command you to live at this level, then we simply must take him seriously because there will be dramatic consequences if we don't. The consequence is not
punishment but rather lack. The Royal Law is to be the restraining influence on our lives. The reason for this is that the keeping of God's commands to love gives us access to obtaining the keys of the kingdom. Of course they are potentially in the hands of every believer but our ability to use them is linked to obedience.

It's time to fully realise who we are in Christ and what we have in Him. As we do, everything will change. We will soon realise that God and not the world is our best chance of success, prosperity, peace, joy and fulfilment. The stipulation placed upon God's Word is not 'experience' it and it will come true; it is 'believe' it and 'act' on it and it will come true. The thing that pleases God the most is when we recognise the integrity of God's word and refuse to pass it through the sieve of sense knowledge. We cannot interpret God through the means of feelings or circumstances.

God asks us to believe Him and it gives Him His greatest joy when we do. Interpretation of facts through sense knowledge belongs to this world because the senses were given so that we could understand our world and thus enlighten the soul. God has not subjected knowledge of Himself to the same means - not at all. He communicates through revelation knowledge. Things that are revealed to us by way of the spirit and the ingredient that allows this to function is, faith expressing itself through love. Hence, the seriousness of the commands to love at God's required, desired level. I have been tested on this many times since it is the nature of the walk. The Royal Law is the answer to living the Christian life and maximising our lives on earth. To secure heaven then maximise your life on earth is not beyond you. It is indeed God's will for you. It is our dream and our vision to help as many people as possible achieve this.

Agape is the most powerful word in the Universe because he has made that word available to all believers. Not just in the sense of imparting understanding and guidance; but also, in our ability to use it as the sword of the Spirit.

It is still able to create and sustain and will do so in our every day lives.

Jesus said, *"whatsoever you bind on earth will be bound in heaven and whatsoever you loose on earth will be loosed in heaven* Matthew 16:19 and 18:18

He meant it, so, do it.

He also said, *"Have faith in God,' Jesus answered. 'Truly I tell you, if anyone says to this mountain, "Go, throw yourself into the sea," and does not doubt in their heart but believes that what they say will happen, it will be done for them. Therefore I tell you, whatever you ask for in prayer, believe that you have received it, and it will be yours. And when you stand praying, if you hold anything against anyone, forgive them, so that your Father in heaven may forgive you your sins."* Mark 11:22-25

The key that unlocks the keys is *agape* in this instance it has its outworking in the following: *"if you hold anything against anyone, forgive them..."*

Once he can trust your heart he will trust you with his supernatural power. The tongue is your greatest weapon; it does indeed hold the power of life and death.

The things that happen to us: circumstances, situations health issues and all are reality. We are not to deny reality but rather attack it with a higher reality.

We can call things that are not (yet) as though they were.

Now let the weak say I am strong. Now let the poor say I am rich.

We are once again in the process of moving to Tanzania. It is over 13 years since we were forced to leave due to my health. What a journey it has been, but we are far better prepared now to fulfil what we are to do in East Africa than we were during our last period here.

A few years after our return to Wales, a stranger approached me at a conference. At this stage, we had been back to Tanzania, many times doing different kinds of ministry, always with a sense of unfinished business. He tapped my shoulder from behind and began with these words,

'God wants you to know, that He is pleased with what you are doing in Africa and fully backs what you're doing.' I looked him in the eye and said,

'Do we know each other?'

'No', he replied.

'Have we met before?' I asked.

'Not to my knowledge,' he answered.

'You've got my attention,' I said, with interest.

He went on to say that God had brought me home to change the rhythm of my heart. I couldn't believe what I was hearing. I asked him if he knew anything about the nature of my sickness that brought us home from Africa. He didn't. I knew that God was speaking to me. My problem had indeed been with the rhythm of my heart. I had 'Arrhythmia'. That was the physical side. However, I knew in an instant that God was talking to me about *agape* (love). The Royal Law of loving God and people at the commanded level is the subject of this book. In the years that have gone by since those dark days of the year 2000, I have become utterly convinced that understanding *agape* is the key of keys and the secret to God's desire and our power. *Agape* is indeed the most powerful word in the Universe. For *agape* **is** God. The Scripture says: God is love (*agape*). They are one and the same.

Agape is the creator.

Agape is the sustainer of all things. Sustaining all things by His powerful word.

The greatest way to succeed is to love your way there.

"If you really keep the royal law found in Scripture, 'Love your neighbour as yourself,' you are doing right." James 2:8

Now we know how to set about doing it. If so, we are going to change our world. An understanding of this will bring about the heart reformation that we so desperately need, leading to the power and authority we have so desperately sought.

May your journey be wonderful and interrupted by miracles every time that you need one.

In the final scenario the Bible tells us that Jesus is coming back to the earth. The following is how he will deals with His enemies,

Revelation 19:15

Coming out of His mouth is a sharp sword with which to strike down the nations.

That is the same power that cursed the fig tree, calmed the storm and brought Lazarus back from the dead. It is the same power that created our world, the same power that sustains our world.

If we live out the law of *agape* we will gain the ability to use the power of *agape*. For the sake of His kingdom may we learn to do this and we too will be able to speak to mountains.

Let's do it.

If you have enjoyed, 'The Most Powerful Word In The Universe.' Please spread the word about it. We have other titles available now.

How to live so you never have to Die – John Bullock

HMS Life – John Bullock

Tears, spaghetti and Angels – D J Bullock

Get your feet off the Table….or you're not going to make it – D J Bullock

Contact us for more details

john@agapelife.co.uk
deb@agapelife.co.uk

To keep up to date with our work in East Africa, you can sign up to receive our newsletter by visiting our website www.agapelife.co.uk

Printed in Poland
by Amazon Fulfillment
Poland Sp. z o.o., Wrocław